Using the *Book of Common Prayer*

A Simple Guide

Paul Thomas

CHURCH HOUSE
PUBLISHING

Church House Publishing
Church House
Great Smith Street
London SW1P 3AZ

Published 2012 by Church House Publishing
Fifth impression 2018
Copyright © Paul Thomas 2012

ISBN 978-0-7151-4276-9

Typeset by Manila Typesetting Company
Printed and bound in England by
CPI Group (UK) Ltd, Croydon

Contents

Preface

Anniversaries are a blessing. The 350th anniversary of the 1662 *Book of Common Prayer* is no exception. It presents us with an opportunity to engage afresh with a founding 'historic formulary' of the Church of England, and to find in it new insights and inspiration. Because of its long and rich history the *Book of Common Prayer* can too easily be regarded as venerable but treated as irrelevant. I hope this simple guide shows that the *Book of Common Prayer* continues to have a power and a place in making Christ known to this generation.

The intention of this book is to encourage a wider use of the *Book of Common Prayer* in the Church today. It attempts this by doing two things: telling the story of the Prayer Book's origins and evolution in an accessible and non-technical way, and providing straightforward practical guidance about how it can be used.

In introducing the story of the *Book of Common Prayer*, I hope I have avoided as much liturgical jargon as possible. The *Book of Common Prayer* should be for all sons and daughters of the Church of England, not only those who are fluent in liturgical lingo. I also hope that in telling its story, others might come to appreciate just how much the Prayer Book expresses the very character of Anglicanism. Conviction and controversy has formed the Prayer Book, so too has both the idealism and the pragmatism of its various compilers. The story of our service book is the story of the Church wrestling to live with the reality of difference, and successfully making a virtue of it.

But this background is only intended to provide sufficient context so that those who lead worship in the Church today might feel that they know the book a little better and so have the confidence to use it a little more. After all, anyone coming to the *Book of Common Prayer* for the first time – especially someone from a non-liturgical background – is bound to feel baffled by it. Getting beyond that bafflement in order to encourage confidence is the intention of this simple guide.

Because of its venerable age, we could easily forget that the *Book of Common Prayer* was in fact revolutionary, and though not the first of its kind it was the best of its kind. That is why it has endured the passing of time where other liturgical books have not. The Prayer Book was revolutionary precisely because it provided, in language fit for memory, a clear, comprehensive, practical and daily guide to praying the Christian life. It also served as a vehicle for bringing to the people what the Reformers sincerely, and with an idealism appropriate to their cause, called 'the pure milk of the Gospel'.

If the *Book of Common Prayer* has survived the generations it has done so because throughout the generations it has been used by different people in different ways, employed with pragmatic flexibility. It is in that spirit that any practical guidance here is given.

Our re-engagement with the *Book of Common Prayer* in its anniversary year has the potential, if we use the opportunity wisely, to inspire us afresh with the converting love of God in Christ that once inspired its compilers.

Paul Thomas
Paddington, May 2012

PART I

A Historical Introduction

The History of the
Book of Common Prayer

The first *Book of Common Prayer* (1549)

Henry, Edward and Reform

Henry VIII died on 28 January 1547. His reign had been long, just two years short of 40, and it had transformed England. A man of massive frame and equally massive personality, Henry had pursued for all of his reign a single policy – the Royal Supremacy. It was his conviction that the Crown should possess 'all honours, dignities, pre-eminencies, jurisdictions, privileges, authorities, immunities, profits and commodities'. This was his driving passion, and he made it the passion of those who surrounded him. Parliament agreed with the King – it dared not disagree – and in November 1534 it passed the first Act of Supremacy, which enshrined in law the rights and claims of the Crown.

A major element of the Royal Supremacy was Henry's control of the Church. The Act stated that Henry was 'the Supreme Head of the Church of England', and to deny that fact was treason. But for all his claims over the Church in his realm, Henry did very little to touch the Church's liturgy. This was because he was not as zealous for liturgical reform as some of his more radical subjects. He was much more the rebellious Catholic than the earnest Reformer, more eager to assert his jurisdiction over the Church in his kingdom than to reform its teachings, customs and services. Henry liked the 'Old Religion'.

His death in January 1547 saw all the 'authorities, dignities and pre-eminences' that he had so energetically acquired for the Crown pass to a boy who was too young and too weak to wear it, Edward VI, Jane Seymour's son.

Henry's will and the Regency Council

Edward's father had left a will. In it, he named 16 executors to care for his son until Edward reached an age when he could rule in his own right, 18 – an age he would never reach. In addition to these 16 executors, a further 18 men were appointed to assist and advise. Together they formed the Regency Council, and between them possessed enormous power. First among them was the young King's uncle, Edward Seymour, who assumed the title Lord Protector of the Realm. But it was a title he held for only a short time. By 1549, Edward Seymour had been replaced with John Dudley (later known as the Duke of Northumberland), who led the Council and guided the King until Edward's early death in 1553. Both these men and most members of the Council were considerably more radical in their desire to see the Church reformed than Henry would ever have allowed in the days of his strength, but in his failing and final years, Henry had seen these reform-minded men gain ever more influence at Court. Thomas Cranmer, Archbishop of Canterbury since 1532, who had been instrumental to Henry in the matter of his divorce ('the King's Great Matter'), was among the members of the Council who hoped that under the new King the Church's worship could be revised and reformed along the lines of the new theology that had so influenced Cranmer and his contemporaries. After all, Cranmer had been labouring since he became Archbishop on a variety of liturgical texts that would soon come together in the *Book of Common Prayer*. As early as the 1530s, the Archbishop of Canterbury had been at work in his study to lay the groundwork for a new English liturgy. Keeping his head down and spending most of each day at his desk (scholarship was his passion, alongside riding), Cranmer had worked in private and with some intensity on texts and services that were soon to become public. But Henry's Archbishop wasn't alone in praying and pressing for change.

The origins of the first *Book of Common Prayer*

The Prayer Book had been some time in the making:

1534
In the same year that the Act of Supremacy enshrined the authority of the King, Convocation (an ancient council of bishops and clergy that met to discuss and decide upon Church affairs) met and petitioned Henry to allow an authorized English translation of the Bible. Until that time, though English Bibles were in circulation, none of them had any official status or sanction. Perhaps the most popular version in circulation at the time was William Tyndale's translation of the New Testament 1525.

1535
Miles Coverdale's translation of the Bible became popular – the Psalms in the *Book of Common Prayer* were to be taken from this translation.

1536
A head of steam was building for the translation of the liturgy into English as well as the Bible. Hugh Latimer preached a sermon at a meeting of Convocation in which he called for the services of Baptism and Holy Matrimony to be conducted entirely in English.

1538
The Bible is placed in every church and the King rules that key liturgical texts should also be used in English: the Creed, the Lord's Prayer and the Ten Commandments. It is also declared that Communion should only be given to those who have learned these texts in English.

1543

Henry continues to ensure the 'good order' of his kingdom by decreeing that 'this realm shall have one Use' ('Use' = service or rite). That Use is to be the medieval services used at Salisbury Cathedral and elsewhere, called the Sarum Use. Alongside the Sarum Use other Uses were being used in different parts of the kingdom – York, Hereford, and Bangor – but it was the Sarum Use that Henry sought to make the standard. As well as pushing for a single liturgical standard across England, the King in 1543 also ordered that a whole chapter from the Bible should be read after the *Te Deum* at Matins and after the *Magnificat* at Evensong each day.

1544

Cranmer produces the Litany in English. The Litany was his translation of the medieval Procession. Processions were a colourful and popular part of medieval devotion. A Procession constituted a separate service that was held outdoors where litanies and prayers would be sung as the procession moved through the streets. Cranmer had been working on an English translation of the Procession for some time. He took the Latin service and did what he did so well, translated it, simplifying and editing it as he went. The amendments he made to the Procession as he translated it are telling; one change that most characterized the growing mood for reform was the significant reduction Cranmer made in the petitions to the saints. Calling on the prayers of the saints had been identified by the Reformers as an 'abuse' and a 'corruption' of worship that they wanted to do away with. Within three years the Litany had largely replaced the Procession, and it was only a few years more before this popular medieval outdoor Procession had been brought within the confines of the parish church and was to be said kneeling.

1547

Henry dies. Edward succeeds his father and the pace of reform picks up. The spirit of reform that Henry's death releases is very much more consciously radical. Edward, however, is not his own man, he is still a minor. The Regency Council looked admiringly to the Continent, especially to Germany and Switzerland, and took inspiration from how the Church had been changed by the new insight of the Reformation and the leadership of such men as Calvin in Geneva, Zwingli in Zurich and Luther in Saxony.

By July 1547, the *Book of Homilies* had been published. It contained short sermons to be read out in churches, sermons that contained teachings and interpretations that were greatly influenced by the continental Reformers. By August, Processions had been banned altogether, and the Epistle and Gospel readings at the Mass were only to be read in English.

1548

The Council banned the rituals and ceremonies surrounding certain popular Holy Days: Candlemas, Ash Wednesday, Palm Sunday. In addition, the Order of Communion was first published. This was not a full service of the Communion but more like a supplement to be used with the Latin Mass. The Order of Communion that Cranmer had been working on provided texts that would eventually find their way in to the first *Book of Common Prayer* and remain there. Alongside the Latin Mass, worshippers were to be given:

- Two exhortations to be read before Communion (to make worshippers receive Communion more devoutly and regularly).
- An invitation to confession, a general confession and the words of absolution.
- The sentences of scripture that would become known as the Comfortable Words.
- The Prayer of Humble Access ('We do not presume to come to this thy table, O merciful Lord . . .').
- The words to be used as Communion was administered ('The Body/Blood of our Lord Jesus Christ which was given/shed for thee . . .').
- The Blessing ('The peace of God which passeth all understanding . . .').

7

The Order of Communion also gave words when a supplementary consecration was needed (more bread and wine), as well as the instruction that the Communion was to be received by people 'in both kinds', which means that people were to receive the cup as well as the bread.

In September 1548, a conference met at Chertsey Abbey. Cranmer was there along with 13 other bishops. At the Chertsey conference, the bishops discussed the texts that were about to be published in a new service book. This book was to be unlike anything that had been published before. It would have within its covers all of the services of the Church – a complete and comprehensive liturgy for the ordained and the lay alike.

Not all the bishops were of the same mind and there was significant disagreement when it came to the Eucharistic doctrine that the *Book of Common Prayer* was teaching. Disagreement erupted again three months later when the Prayer Book was debated in Parliament. When it came to the vote, ten bishops voted in favour of the new services, eight against. The bishops were divided between Evangelicals and Catholics.

1549

On 21 January the first Act of Uniformity was passed by Parliament. For the first time, it gave legal force to a single liturgy, the first *Book of Common Prayer*. Failure to use the *Book of Common Prayer* from Pentecost that year (9 June) became a criminal offence. The Act left no doubt about the status of the new liturgy: 'If any parson [or other minister] refused to use the said common prayers . . . he shall be thereof legally convicted according to the laws of this Realm.'

Parliament went on to make its expectations clear:

All single ministers within this realm . . . shall from after the feast of Pentecost next coming, be bound to say and use the Matins, Evensong, celebration of the Lord's Supper, commonly called the Mass, and administration of each of the Sacraments, and all their common and open prayers, in such order and form as is mentioned in the said book and none other or otherwise.

Times were changing.

The principles behind the Prayer Book

The project to produce a comprehensive service book for the Church of England had been driven by those at the heart of the political establishment who wanted to bring to England the benefits of Church reform by which Cranmer had been so influenced on the Continent. But in order for the new book to be received and understood, it needed to be justified and explained. To do this, Cranmer wrote a Preface to the first *Book of Common Prayer* that set out the underlying principles of the book. The 1549 Preface soon became a classic statement of Anglican liturgical principles, and it has been reprinted in every version of the Prayer Book since 1549.

Stirred to Godliness

Cranmer's intention was serious and devout; he was earnestly and evangelically working to create a Christian society, one that he believed would come about when 'the very pure word of God' was brought to the people of England. Everyone influenced by the spirit of the Reformation had come to appreciate that a new and closer engagement with the scriptures was essential to salvation and to living the Christian life. Cranmer understood the scriptures as the touchstone of all truth and authority in the Church. That is why he stated in the Preface that 'the first and original ground' of the liturgy was so that the scriptures could be read in good order. Cranmer quotes the authority of 'the ancient Fathers' for his argument that from the very earliest days the liturgy was intended to allow 'all the whole Bible' to be 'read over once a year'. By reading the scriptures in this way, the clergy would be 'stirred up to Godliness themselves and so be more able to exalt others by wholesome doctrine'. The new Prayer Book, then, was to be a framework of liturgy in which the scriptures were to be read, heard and learned by men and women, lay and ordained, so that they 'might continually profit more and more in the knowledge of God and be more inflamed with the love of his true Religion'. The first Prayer Book was part of a programme to introduce and educate the people of England in the saving truths of scripture.

Plain and easy to be understood

Cranmer's great concern was that when the Bible was read in church it was rarely understood by the hearer or even by the reader. Latin services were characterized as incomprehensible: 'they have heard with their ears only, their heart, spirit and mind have not been edified thereby'. His new service book would remove the 'multitude of Responds, Verses, vain Repetitions, Commemorations and Synodals'. The Bible in the new Prayer Book would also be read consistently for the first time, since some books were 'only begun and never read through'. Cranmer's vision was to bring the whole of the Bible into the lives of the English. Because simplifying, unifying, translating and reforming was Cranmer's agenda, a calendar (a table of what scripture passages should be read and when – lectionary) was provided so that 'all things shall be done in order'. This would ensure 'the continual course of reading scripture'.

All the whole Realm shall have but one Use

The Tudors liked order and they feared chaos. Establishing a single Use, therefore, was important for the unity and stability of the Church and kingdom. Initially that had been the Sarum Use, but now it was to be the *Book of Common Prayer* that would provide the desired clarity and uniformity. Cranmer assured the clergy that they 'shall need no other books for their public service but this book and the Bible'. Services had suddenly become simpler. For Cranmer, this was as much a pastoral imperative as a liturgical one. His reform of the Church had a very practical dimension too, not only bringing the gospel closer to the people but providing the clergy with the means of ministering to their people more directly and effectively.

Of Ceremonies

We have to remember that the religious practice of Cranmer's day was highly ceremonial. The argument that many Reformers put forward was that these ceremonies had become so complex and numerous that they obscured and detracted from the worship of almighty God. If the Preface set out the basic liturgical principles behind the new service book, 'Of Ceremonies' touched on why certain ceremonies 'be abolished and some retained'. Cranmer was more concerned that words spoke louder than actions, but nevertheless certain actions were retained in the new Prayer Book. Even though so much of the Reformation in England was inspired by a conscious moving away from visual modes of communication and towards the written and spoken word, there was still a place for certain ceremonies (only if they served to enhance the gospel message of salvation).

Used or left as every man's duty serveth

Cranmer's assessment of Church ceremonies reflects the suspicions and objections of many Reformers. He identifies three orders of ceremonies within the Church:

- Ceremonies that 'at the first were of Godly intent and purpose devised, and yet at length turned to vanity and superstition'. These customs and ceremonies are to be done away with.

- Other ceremonies 'entered in by undiscreet devotion and with such a zeal as without knowledge [with the result that they] grew daily to more and more abuses'. These abuses had 'much blinded' the people and 'obscured the glory of God and are worthy to be cut away'.
- The third category of ceremonies Cranmer is more sympathetic to because 'although they have been devised by man, yet it is thought good to rescue them still as well for decent order in the Church'. Continuing certain ceremonies is acceptable 'because they pertain to edification'. 'Edification' is, for Cranmer, his priority. It is a word he uses time and again to explain the basis for his liturgical reforms. In the Archbishop's vocabulary, it meant to be educated, stirred to a deeper devotion through knowledge and 'sound doctrine'.

All of this makes the Prayer Book intentionally ceremony-lite. The *Book of Common Prayer* includes only a few ceremonies as essential to its services (for example signing with the sign of the cross at Baptism, the use of the ring in marriage), because for Cranmer rituals and ceremonies do not have the authority of God's law and so can be retained or omitted as necessary. His suspicion of anything 'instituted by man' was a suspicion shared by many Protestants at the time. Cranmer was convinced by the fallenness of humanity and therefore the fallenness of the human customs and traditions that had made their way into the Church.

New fangled and old

The concerns and the passions of the Reformers were to purify the medieval Church of what they saw as distortions of the truth. However, even though the changes that Cranmer brought about in England were radical, they were still significantly more conservative than some had hoped for and less radical than other examples of Reformation on the Continent. Naturally cautious and highly principled,

Cranmer understood that if unity was to be maintained in the kingdom he could not push too far or too fast in this first phase of reform. For that reason he is critical in the Preface of those who 'be so new fangled that they would innovate all things, and so despise the old, that nothing can like them, but that is new'. Those who love this 'new fangled' religion are told that some of the inherited customs 'do serve to a decent order and Godly discipline' and are 'apt to stir up the dull mind of man to the remembrance of his duty to God, by some notable and special signification'. A measure of ritual therefore was deliberately retained in the *Book of Common Prayer*, partly because Cranmer was a student of as well as a product of the medieval tradition, and partly because he saw the value of compromise. His new service book would take a moderate Reformation into the country.

Both the Preface and Of Ceremonies taken together tell us a great deal about the author of the Prayer Book, his priorities, and the product of his labours. This was a book driven by a clear intention to rationalize and reform the English Church in a way that introduced the new theology of the Reformation but which consciously avoided extremes of opinion. For the sake of 'good order' the *Book of Common Prayer* attempted a balance between continuity and change, between reverence for antiquity and the insights of the new theology. It was an exercise in compromise. This balance – which is now accepted as a fundamental characteristic of Anglicanism – was neatly summed up in a phrase found in 'Certain Notes', which was published at the back of the first Prayer Book. It happens to be discussing the use of gestures in worship, but a wider principle is at work in it. In recognition of the different ritual practices of Christians in England, Cranmer composed a rubric that encapsulated the Prayer Book's spirit of moderation: 'touching kneeling, crossing, holding up of hands, knocking upon the breast, and other gestures; they may be used or left as every man's devotion serveth without blame'. The reform of the liturgy was both highly principled and sensibly pragmatic.

The contents of the first Prayer Book (1549)

The first *Book of Common Prayer* was published on 7 March 1549 by Edward Whitchurch, and its contents page listed the services it contained. These services were intended to cover every possible liturgical and pastoral occasion.

Contents

1 A Preface.

2 A Table and Calendar of Psalms and Lessons with necessary rules pertaining to the same.

3 The Order for Matins and Evensong, throughout the year.

4 The Introits, Collects, Epistles and Gospels to be used at the celebration of the Lord's Supper and Holy Communion throughout the year, with proper Psalms and Lessons, for divers, feasts and days.

5 The Supper of the Lord and Holy Communion, commonly called The Mass.

6 Of Baptism, both public and private.

7 Of Confirmation, where also there is a Catechism for children.

8 Of Matrimony.

9 Of Visitation of the Sick, and Communion of the same.

10 Of Burial.

11 The Purification of Women.

12 A Declaration of Scripture, with certain prayers to be used on the first day of Lent, commonly called Ash Wednesday.

13 Of Ceremonies omitted and retained.

14 Certain Notes for the more plain explanation, and decent ministration of things contained in this book.

The contents page makes it clear that this book was intended to take a Christian from cradle to grave. It provided the liturgical materials for the celebration of each Sunday of the

Christian year as well as the highly significant innovation of two daily services, Matins and Evensong. Although Cranmer was not unique in doing this (several other authors at the time were composing shortened daily services for use by clergy and laity alike), the daily services of Matins and Evensong are the lynchpin of his liturgical reforms. Daily services were to be essential in realizing the goal of a Christian society where men and women grew in holiness by sharing in common prayer and the reading of the scriptures each day.

Preface

The Preface sets out the need for reform and the principles underlining that reform. It has become a classic statement of Anglican liturgical principles.

Table and Calendar

Because the scriptures take a central place in the new services and are to be read in full not in part, the Calendar sets out how this is to be done – every day, in English, in its entirety. In Cranmer's new system, the Bible was no longer to be read selectively or in piecemeal. In the Calendar Cranmer devised, *lectio continua* (continuous reading of scripture) was chosen in favour of *lectio selecta* (selective reading of scripture). This was achieved by a simple system that meant that the Old Testament was divided up in such a way that it was read in its entirety once each year, the New Testament three times in a year, and the Psalter once every month.

Matins and Evensong

These services are Cranmer's lasting achievement. Matins and Evensong (Morning and Evening Prayer) have become the staple diet for generations of Anglicans worldwide. Strongly influenced by the medieval world that he knew, Cranmer drew heavily on the medieval monastic services of his time when composing Matins and Evensong. Matins was a skilful knitting together of three of the nine monastic daily services (Matins, Lauds and Prime), which took place in the early morning. Evensong was made up of the last two services of the monastic day (Vespers and Compline). By editing, simplifying and translating the tradition of monastic daily prayer into two services, Cranmer hoped to instruct and 'edify' the laity and give them much greater access to worship than ever before.

Introits and Collects

For each Sunday and each feast day the Prayer Book provided Propers (readings and prayers specific to the particular day). In doing this, Cranmer took the opportunity to reduce significantly the number of feast days and saints' days that had been popularly celebrated. In a mark of continuity with Catholic worship, introits (introductory sentences of scripture) were included in the propers for the Communion. However, where the medieval services provided only a single sentence, usually from the Psalms, Cranmer provided for the entire Psalm to be read. Here is an example of how he and his fellow Reformers worked hard at every turn to ensure that scripture was at the centre of the liturgy, that the integrity of the Bible was maintained and the authority of the Bible reinforced.

Holy Communion

The most significant and sensitive element in any liturgical reform is the reform of the eucharistic liturgy. Cranmer approached his reform with care and subtlety. He wanted the Prayer Book to show both sufficient continuity and sufficient change – a tightrope that he walked with some skill.

Cranmer was persuaded by reformed arguments about the Eucharist. These arguments centred on the rejection of Transubstantiation (the belief that the essence of the bread and wine was changed in the Eucharist to become the very body and blood of Christ), and the sacrificial character of the medieval

Mass (the popular belief that the Mass in some way repeated Christ's own sacrifice). Mindful, however, of how traditional popular devotion was, the changes Cranmer introduced are intentional but subtle. For example, the priest would continue to celebrate from an altar, the *Kyrie* and the *Gloria in excelsis* would continue in their usual place at the beginning of the Mass, the collects and readings were almost entirely taken from the medieval service, the celebrant continued to be described as the 'priest' and the traditional language of 'chalice' and 'paten' was used. The Prayer of Consecration was retained as the central act of the service in which the saints were invoked and the departed commemorated.

In many ways, the outward appearance of the Communion in the first *Book of Common Prayer* was very similar to what had gone before, even if it was no longer in Latin. However, subtle steps were being taken to reform the Church's beliefs about the Eucharist by the changes that Cranmer introduced. For example, the rite was now entirely in English, a prayer for the monarch was to be said before the Collect for the Day, the sermon or homily was given new prominence, and exhortations were included to encourage worshippers to receive communion devoutly.

The Prayer of Consecration may have appeared familiar, but even there Cranmer was at work reforming the Church's Eucharistic doctrine. He inserted an Epiclesis (invocation of the Holy Spirit over the bread and cup), which was very unusual for its time. The Epiclesis is now a familiar feature in Eucharistic Prayers in the twentieth century, but it was a rare thing in the sixteenth century. Why did he introduce it? Perhaps it shows the breadth of the Archbishop's learning (he spent two thirds of each day in study and possessed one of the finest libraries of his generation) or perhaps it makes an appeal to the Orthodox Churches and the liturgical practice of the Church Fathers and the earlier centuries of the Church. It was certainly Cranmer's stated conviction that his new Prayer Book should recapture the teaching and practice of the 'Primitive Church' (the Church at the time of the Apostles and early Christians). The invocation of the Holy Spirit over the bread and cup of the Eucharist was evidence that something 'primitive' and authentic was being recovered in the Church of England through these liturgical reforms.

Significantly, one of the ceremonies that Cranmer did away with was the elevation of the eucharistic elements. In a rubric in the *Book of Common Prayer*, the Archbishop gave this direction: 'these words [this is my body . . . this is my blood . . .] before rehearsed are to be said, turning still to the altar, without any elevation, or showing the Sacrament to the people'. This minor change was a major reform. The central act to the medieval Mass, the moment that those attending the Mass had come to witness, was the consecration of the bread and cup by the priest using the dominical words ('this is my body . . . this is my blood . . .'). Medieval theology taught that the tradition of saying Christ's words over the bread and cup by the priest was the moment of consecration. When the priest said the dominical words, then the bread and wine became Christ's very body and blood. Those consecrated elements were then elevated for all to see. It was an important and highly visual moment.

By something as simple as forbidding the elevation, Cranmer was making a statement. He was saying that the doctrine of transubstantiation was being downplayed or even rejected. By denying the people the opportunity to see the Eucharistic elements at the moment of their consecration was in effect to diminish or even deny the miracle by which they became the very body and blood of Christ.

Following the Prayer of Consecration (or what today we would call the Eucharistic Prayer), was the Lord's Prayer. Following that were the liturgical texts that had been introduced into the Latin Mass only a year earlier under the Order for Communion – the Comfortable Words and the Prayer of Humble Access.

Baptism

The Baptism service, typical of the other services in the Prayer Book, was closely based on the medieval service books that Cranmer then significantly simplified. He introduced exhortations to the service in which the duties and responsibilities of the parents and Godparents of the child were spelled out for the first time. These were composed by Cranmer's friend and fellow theologian Martin Bucer. But there were as many continuities as there were changes in the new Prayer Book. The Baptism service continued to have features of the medieval rite, for example oil was still used to anoint the head and breast of the child before Baptism. This was a continuity that many of Cranmer's more radical colleagues opposed. In addition, both the exorcism and robing of the child in a white garment (this was called the 'crysome') were continued.

Confirmation

The significant reform in this service was the removal of the rite of anointing that, until then, had been the central moment of confirmation. While the Prayer Book service had many similarities to the medieval service, Cranmer took advantage of his translation to reinterpret confirmation in a way that has had a lasting effect on the Anglican tradition.

In the Middle Ages, confirmation had been administered by a bishop who conferred God's grace on a candidate by the laying on of hands. Cranmer moved the meaning of confirmation so that the emphasis now fell on 'edification' – his notion that people should grow in their personal faith by growing in knowledge and understanding of 'true Religion'.

His intention is set out in the long rubric (guidance note) at the beginning of the service. Confirmation was intended for children who had 'come to the years of discretion and have learned what their Godfathers and Godmothers promised for them in Baptism . . . [that they] may themselves with their own mouth, and with their own consent openly before the church ratify and confess the same'. Candidates for confirmation in this new service were being given the opportunity to confess their own faith. Personal affirmation became the focus of confirmation in the *Book of Common Prayer*. In this way, the service was given greater prominence than before, because it encouraged candidates, in a Church where all members were being encouraged to participate more personally in the worship of God and to understand the truths of their religion, to 'endeavour themselves to observe and keep' their confession of faith. In order to help the children of the Church of England grow in knowledge and understanding (and so in 'godliness'), a Catechism was provided for the first time.

Catechism

The new Catechism was subtitled 'An instruction to be learned of every child before he be brought to be confirmed by the bishop'. Among other things, it was intended to instruct children in the 'articles of thy faith'. By this was meant the Apostles' Creed (which was provided with a brief explanation) and the Ten Commandments. Cranmer was determined that the children raised according to his new Prayer Book were to be literate in their religion and faithful in their duty to God, their neighbour, and their king. When asked in the Catechism, 'What is thy duty towards thy neighbour?', the answer was: 'to love . . . my father and mother. To honour and obey the King and his ministers . . . to order myself lowly and reverently to all my betters'. It was characteristic of Cranmer and the English Reformation to marry godliness with obedience.

Matrimony

Cranmer was the first Archbishop of Canterbury to marry. In fact, he married a second time after his first wife died. The Marriage service in his new Prayer Book drew heavily on its medieval predecessor. That too contained a provision for the vows to be said in English not Latin, and those vows were incorporated by Cranmer with only minor changes.

The new service was to be conducted in 'the body of the church', not at the porch or door as had been the earlier custom (it was typical of the English Reformation to want to contain and authorize religious activity by bringing it within the walls of the parish church). In the Preface read by the priest, marriage is defined as 'an honourable estate instituted of God in paradise', and therefore not strictly a sacrament (evidence of the Reformers' intention to diminish the sacramental character of services that weren't Communion or Baptism). Following it came the declarations and vows. The giving of the ring was retained, as were the 'other tokens of spousage as gold and silver'. The continued use of the ring in the Marriage service dissatisfied many who wished to see it reformed out of existence. It was assumed in the 1549 Prayer Book that the Marriage service would be followed immediately by the celebration of Holy Communion, though the rubric leaves some room for flexibility: 'the new married persons (the same day of their marriage) must receive the Holy Communion'.

Visitation of the Sick

This service provided a number of liturgical materials for use in the home or at the bedside of a sick person. The sick person was greeted with a Psalm (Psalm 143) and after a short verse and response, a series of collects. A long exhortation followed, with the provision for it to be longer if necessary. The Apostles' Creed, which is used frequently in the Prayer Book, was to be said by the sick person 'as it is in Baptism', and an opportunity was given for the sick person to put his affairs in order – both spiritual and domestic. The individual is encouraged to undertake self-examination, put worldly goods in order, if necessary write a will, declare any debts, and show 'liberality to the poor'. Significantly, the service also provides for 'the sick person to make a special confession if he feel his conscience troubled with any weighty matter'. This opportunity for confession is provided with an absolution with the note that 'the same form of absolution shall be used in all private confessions'. Following a further Psalm, anthem and collect, the guidance notes allow for the sick person to be anointed 'upon the forehead and the breast only, making the sign of the Cross'. The service ends with a prayer for recovery and pardon, and a thanksgiving for triumph 'against thine adversary', and a Psalm.

Communion of the Sick

The private celebration of Communion was a sensitive subject for the Reformers because they feared that it was open to all kinds of 'abuses'. They wanted it stopped. At the same time they recognized the need for Communion at home in the case of the sick. That is why the visitation of the sick in the first Prayer Book gives extensive guidance on how this should be done. In keeping with the pastoral and theological principles of Cranmer and his colleagues, a short service for the sick to receive Communion was provided in the first Prayer Book. A long rubric provides guidance on how and when the sick might receive the sacrament. This lengthy rubric makes it clear that 'if the sick person be not able to come to the church and yet is desirous to receive the Communion in his house', then he must inform the 'curate' in advance. If there is an 'open Communion' in the church that day then the priest will reserve the sacrament 'and shall serve the sick person'. This is done in the home by saying the confession, receiving absolution, hearing the 'comfortable sentences' and ending with a Prayer of Thanksgiving for Holy Communion. Yet if there is no 'open Communion' in church, the Prayer Book makes provision for Communion to be celebrated in the home of the sick person. If the sick cannot receive because of illness, then a rubric is provided. It has also become a key element of Anglican pastoral theology:

If he do truly repent him of his sins, and steadfastly believe that Jesus Christ hath suffered death upon the Cross for him, and shed his blood for his redemption, earnestly remembering the benefits he hath thereby, and giving him hearty thanks therefore: he doth eat and drink spiritually the body and blood of our Saviour Christ, although he doth not receive the Sacrament with his mouth.

Burial

The popular customs surrounding death and the dead worried the Reformers, who had come to challenge the medieval Church's teaching about the departed. Prayer for the departed was held up by Cranmer as an example of how distorted and superstitious the Church's faith had become over time. The Reformers dedicated themselves to suppressing and overturning these traditional beliefs and customs surrounding death. Their objection was based on their belief that salvation was by faith alone and not works, and only through a 'lively faith' in Jesus Christ could anyone be saved. Praying for the departed was a corruption of the true faith, they argued, because it assumed that God could be persuaded to look favourably on the departed even if their life was not godly. It offended the Reformers' belief in the supreme freedom of God and their belief that God had predestined some souls to life and others to damnation (a popular Calvinist belief called Double Predestination).

Unsurprisingly, the Burial service as it appeared in the Prayer Book was dramatically slimmed down in comparison to the Latin service. The new liturgy only allowed for a service in church and then at the grave, or a service at the graveside followed by a short service in church. The rite is brief and very biblical, and includes a prayer commending the dead by name to God. A second prayer follows that prays for 'his soul and all the souls of thy elect'. The Reformed theology of the elect is never far from Cranmer's mind. Those whom God had preordained to be saved were described as 'the elect'.

In recognition of the popular place that the Requiem Mass played in medieval devotion, but against Cranmer's Evangelical instincts, the Prayer Book still included the necessary liturgical texts for a celebration of the Communion in church following the burial. But where one thing is given another is taken away – the Prayer Book removes from the service any prayer for the departed and any reference to purgatory. The old and the new religion were living uneasily side by side.

The Purification of Women

This brief service in the *Book of Common Prayer* was a reworking of the medieval service that in turn was inspired by the Jewish rite of purification, hence its biblical name in the 1549 Prayer Book. It consisted of a short introduction typical of so many services of the Reformation period, explaining the intention of the service. A Psalm was provided to be said by the priest and the woman. After a brief litany, the priest says a collect praying for the woman to 'faithfully live and walk in her vocation' according to God's will. This short service ends with a direction that the purified woman 'must offer her crysome and other accustomed offerings', and allows for the service to lead into the Communion. 'Crysome' refers to the ancient custom where the white robe of baptism was brought back to the church for the act of purification. The 'accustomed offerings' likely refer to the offertory at the Communion that followed when the mother was expected to give to the church a gift in thanksgiving for the safe deliverance of her and her child from 'the great pain and peril of childbirth'.

The First Day of Lent

The ancient Ash Wednesday ceremonies were outlawed in 1548. However, the title of this service recognizes the enduring significance of the old name 'Ash Wednesday'. This service, which later became known as the Commination, was drawn from the pre-Reformation service, being amended and significantly reduced in length. The introduction was composed for this new liturgy. It was followed by 'the general sentences of God's cursing against impenitent sinners' taken from Deuteronomy 27. A second extended address by the minister drew heavily on biblical quotations and is followed by the curses. These in turn lead to Psalm 51 and the collect.

Publication and rebellion

The Act of Uniformity that enshrined the *Book of Common Prayer* in the law of the land became law on 21 January 1549 after a troubled passage through Parliament. Nearly half the bishops had voted against it. This didn't bode well for how the new service book would be received in the country at large. Its passage through Parliament was significant for another reason. It was the first time Parliament had decided what the Church's liturgy should be. Henry's Act of Supremacy 15 years earlier had successfully brought the Church under the authority of the Crown. Lay not ecclesiastical power was first in the land, and the Church's worship was to be governed not by Convocation but by the Crown and Parliament.

The divisions in Parliament over the *Book of Common Prayer* pointed to deep divisions in the country. Pentecost was the appointed date for the launch of the new book and local magistrates were given the responsibility to enforce its use. In Cornwall and Devon, however, Pentecost did not bring harmony and concord but protest and conflict.

The Prayer Book Rebellion of 1549

The Prayer Book Rebellion is the name given to a series of uprisings in the West Country between June and August 1549 in protest at the new liturgy. The uprisings were serious enough for Edward VI's uncle to despatch in the name of his nephew troops to suppress the protests. The grievance of the rebels was that the new liturgy had replaced the old rites, and that too many old customs had been done away with in the process. They demanded the restoration of Catholic worship and described Cranmer's new services as 'lyke a Christmas game'. Protestors laid siege to Exeter to prove the strength of their feeling.

The Regency Council moved quickly to challenge the rebels, responding to their criticisms of the new *Book of Common Prayer* with the claim that the new liturgies were not so very different from the old ones: 'It seemeth to you a new service, and indeed it is none other than the old' they said in a message to the Cornish rebels. It's questionable whether this statement was ever sincerely meant. After all, the Regency Council would have felt the first *Book of Common Prayer* to be too conservative for their reforming tastes. Nevertheless, they felt that the riots in the West Country would be more effectively disbanded with the assurance that not much had changed.

In addition to the movement to return to the Latin Mass, traditional vestments, customs and teachings, the protestors objected to the use of English: 'We the Cornish men whereof certain of us understand no English, utterly refuse this new English.' Not everyone had fallen in love with Cranmer's polished way with words, and 5,000 rebels died in defying the imposition of the new Prayer Book.

Critics at home and abroad

The Cornish were not alone in reacting against the *Book of Common Prayer*. The first Prayer Book had barely been published before it was receiving criticism. Reformers on and from the Continent had eagerly awaited the new service book, which they hoped would be as radical if not more so as the Lutheran service books in Germany, but they were disappointed.

When John Calvin (1509–64), whose own reform of the Church in Geneva was held by many modernizers as the only model to follow, saw Cranmer's service book, he didn't think much of it. In a letter, Calvin commented on the Prayer Book's 'many tolerable absurdities'. He was not alone. Others criticized its conservatism. Martin Bucer (1491–1551) was a friend and fellow traveller with Cranmer. His *Censura*, published in 1551, listed the *Book of Common Prayer*'s many liturgical and doctrinal shortcomings – 60 in total. Peter Martyr (1499–1562), another eminent Reformation theologian and Regius

Professor of Divinity at Oxford, added his voice to the chorus of criticism. Reformers at home and abroad had been looking and hoping for something much more radical, and Bucer's 60 criticisms of the Prayer Book made that clear. The problem with Cranmer's service book was that it was too conservative for radicals and too radical for conservatives.

This must have come as a blow to Cranmer, who had been working on the texts for the *Book of Common Prayer* for some years. Martin Bucer's criticism was particularly sharp. Bucer had been invited from Germany to England by Cranmer himself in 1549, being received by the Archbishop with great personal warmth and formal ceremony on his arrival in England. Bucer's greatest contribution to the Church's liturgical reforms proved to be the Ordinal (Ordination Services), which is largely his own work, published the year after the first Prayer Book.

The Prayer Book also had its critics from among Cranmer's fellow bishops. The more radical English bishops, such as John Hooper (Bishop of Gloucester) and Nicholas Ridley (Bishop of Worcester), fiercely criticized the new Prayer Book as too limited and timid in its reforms. In Hooper's case, he had spent two years living in Zurich and had come under the influence of the Swiss Reformers Zwingli and Bullinger. Hooper's zeal for the far-reaching liturgical reforms he found among the Alps led him to look on the Prayer Book with disappointment and even disgust.

Criticism not only came from Evangelical quarters. Catholic bishops and clergy also expressed their opposition to some of the innovations that the first Prayer Book introduced. The leading bishops who challenged Cranmer's reforms and the agenda of Edward VI's Protestant Council were Stephen Gardiner (Bishop of Winchester) and Edmund Bonner (Bishop of London). Both of them had been instrumental in asserting the Royal Supremacy under Henry VIII. By 1549, however, they found themselves in opposition to the way that the Supremacy was being wielded by the new King's counsellors. Bonner refused to be present at St Paul's Cathedral when the Archbishop of

Canterbury preached there on Pentecost 1549 (later that year Bonner was deposed). Stephen Gardiner applied an altogether different approach and damned the *Book of Common Prayer* with faint praise by claiming that the new Prayer Book just about preserved the essentials of the Latin Mass, a claim that so irritated Thomas Cranmer that it led to a very public dispute between them in print.

In the months following Pentecost 1549, the criticisms only mounted. It was becoming clear that the momentum for further change was growing, and that those who hoped for a more Reformed Prayer Book were soon to have their way.

The second *Book of Common Prayer* (1552)

Catholic bishops and clergy stood in firm opposition to the elements of evangelical theology implicit in the new Prayer Book, whereas evangelical bishops and clergy condemned it for its limited ambition to bring about the changes for which they longed. This meant that although the first Prayer Book had taken years to compose, its life was to be short and three years later it was superseded by a second Prayer Book. Many in the wider population seemed committed to the old traditions and customs of faith, others hardly noticed the changes where they were only selectively implemented, but the new theological insights of the Reformation had succeeded in persuading educated men of the middle and merchant classes that further reform was essential. To those now at the centre of the Tudor State, the Tudor Church still bore too many resemblances to its medieval predecessor.

Where did Cranmer stand in all of this? The author of the first Prayer Book seems to have felt little loyalty to his creation. Indeed, it appears that no sooner was the ink dry on the 1549 *Book of Common Prayer* than work had commenced on its successor.

The criticisms the first book had received, for example kneeling at communion, continued use of eucharistic vestments, prayers for the dead and anointing at baptism, were accurate reflections of Cranmer's own increasingly evangelical position towards outward ceremonies and their inward meaning. The Bishop of London, Nicholas Ridley, was one such evangelical influence on Cranmer. Ridley had enthusiastically engaged in the policy of reform in his own diocese by working hard to remove as many stone altars as he could. Cranmer was also being egged on by the accumulated opinion of continental theologians whose company he kept and whose opinions he valued. This meant that even by 1548 the Archbishop of Canterbury had become less German and more Swiss, less Lutheran and more Calvinist in his theological convictions. One of the many differences between the German and Swiss Reformations was the extent to which the outward ordering of worship had been altered. In Germany, many of the altars had remained in place and the appearance of worship had remained much the same. In Zurich, however, where Zwingli had reformed the Church and in Geneva where Calvin had done the same, a much more radical approach had been taken. The service books of the German Reformation were consciously traditional in comparison with the Swiss preference for a lengthy sermon with certain Psalms and prayers attached. This difference in approach towards the liturgy reflected a different way of reading and receiving the Bible. Generally speaking, Lutherans were content to keep the old customs unless God's law revealed in scripture stated otherwise. Zwingli and Calvin, however, urged an interpretation of scripture that said that whatever was not explicitly stated in the Bible must be a human imposition and therefore must be rejected.

In the late 1540s, Cranmer was leaning evermore in the direction of Zurich and Geneva and to the examples of Church reform that they offered. 'Praise God' wrote an enthusiastic follower of Zwingli to his friend and fellow Reformer, Bullinger, in September 1548. 'Latimer has come over to our doctrine of the Eucharist and so has the Archbishop of Canterbury and other bishops who until now had seemed Lutheran.'

The Eucharistic doctrine in question was one that rejected the real presence of Christ in the Eucharist and instead saw the Eucharist as a memorial meal.

These convictions weren't Cranmer's alone. They were shared by those who guided and advised the King – the Regency Council. A further liturgical revision was needed, they felt, and it was in Edward's name and by his authority that it would be undertaken.

In April 1552, Parliament passed the second Act for Uniformity. This gave the latest Prayer Book the force of law. It also made refusal to use it a criminal offence. The question remains how many people actually ever used the 1552 *Book of Common Prayer*, because it was published so soon after the first book and was itself only used for a matter of months before it too was abolished. Nevertheless, there was a concerted effort by churchmen and statesmen alike to establish the second Prayer Book and to establish the doctrine it taught. The second *Book of Common Prayer* was issued in the winter of 1552.

The contents of the second Book of Common Prayer *(1552)*

The second *Book of Common Prayer* was different from the first in a number of ways. Its character was much more Protestant. Even the name of the book was altered to reflect the change of mood. In 1549, the *Book of Common Prayer* had been officially called 'The *Book of Common Prayer* and Administration of the Sacraments, and other Rites and Ceremonies of the Church after the use of the Church of England'. The new book's title removed reference to the wider Church of which the Church of England was part in order to stress the Church of England's separation from the pre-Reformation Church. In 1552, it was called 'The *Book of Common Prayer* and Administration of the Sacraments, and other Rites and Ceremonies in the Church of England'. A national Protestant Church was being consciously created, defined in and through a new more Protestant liturgy. But it was behind the front cover that the most significant changes were found.

Morning and Evening Prayer

The medieval names Matins and Evensong were dropped in favour of Morning and Evening Prayer. This made a clear break with the monastic and pre-Reformation origins of these services.

Morning and Evening Prayer were to be said 'in such a place in the church that the people may best hear', whereas the 1549 *Book of Common Prayer* stated that Matins and Evensong should be said 'in the choir', a change that further emphasized the separation between the monastic office and these new services.

New rubrics (guidance notes) relating to Morning Prayer made it clear that the priest would appear differently from before because he 'should use neither alb, vestment or cope' but surplice only. The Ornaments Rubric of 1549 had given official sanction for a variety of priestly garments to be worn for services in the new Prayer Book. This was now abolished.

The Penitential Sentences from the Bible and the long Penitential Introduction were added in 1552. This consisted of the bidding, a Confession for the congregation to say together (General Confession), an Absolution, and the Lord's Prayer.

Holy Communion

In the 1552 Prayer Book, Communion was called the 'Order for the administration of the Lord's Supper or Holy Communion'. 'Commonly called the Mass' was removed.

A new rubric referring to the place and appearance of the 'large table' was clearly intended to change in people's minds the place where Communion was celebrated. The Catholic altar was now a Protestant table that 'shall stand in the body of the church or in the Chancel'. The priest was directed to stand 'at the north side of the table' and not 'in the midst' as in the 1549 *Book of Common Prayer*.

The *Kyries* (Lord, have mercy upon us) were replaced by the Ten Commandments. This brought the 1552 *Book of Common Prayer* more into line with certain continental service books.

The *Gloria* was moved from the beginning to the end of the service in order to make Communion more obviously different from the medieval service.

Several of the salutations 'the Lord be with you' were also removed, but it was in the Prayer of Consecration where the most significant change took place. The long prayer, often called the Canon of the Mass, had been a single movement in the 1549 Prayer Book. In 1552 it was divided into five different parts:

- 'The Prayer for Christ's Church' was separated from the Prayer of Consecration, brought forward in the service, and renamed 'The Prayer for Christ's Church Militant here in Earth'. This was done to reinforce the belief that prayers should no longer be offered for the departed (often called 'the Church Expectant') or to the saints (called 'the Church Triumphant').
- All prayers for the departed were removed.
- The Exhortations changed their place in the service. In the 1552 *Book of Common Prayer*, they were placed within what had been the Prayer of Consecration in order to disrupt its flow.
- Confession and Absolution were also repositioned and placed within what had been the Prayer of Consecration.
- The Prayer of Humble Access was moved to a position after the *Sursum Corda* ('Lift up your hearts'), whereas in the 1549 *Book of Common Prayer* it had come after the consecration and immediately before receiving communion.
- The Prayer of Consecration was significantly shortened to consist almost entirely of the institution narrative (the story of the Last Supper) and the words of institution ('this is my body . . . this is my blood . . .'). To further diminish the prominence of the consecration, the prayer did not even end with 'Amen'.

All these changes were motivated by a conviction that the Prayer of Consecration (indeed the whole of the service of Communion) needed to be slimmed down and stripped away so that it closely and consciously resembled the Last Supper itself. Thomas Cranmer is deliberately trying to recapture what he believed was the authentic pattern of the earliest Eucharist. That is why the second Prayer Book, with its strong Protestant influence, asserts that nothing more than the words of Jesus Christ were sufficient for Communion to be celebrated because ultimately what mattered was the faith of the one receiving Communion, not the words and ceremonies surrounding the celebration of the sacrament.

Changing the words by which Communion was celebrated was of great importance for the Reformers, but so too were the words by which Communion was given. The words of administration from the 1549 *Book of Common Prayer* had allowed a belief in the real presence of Christ in the Eucharist: 'The body/ blood of our Lord Jesus Christ which was given/shed for thee, preserve thy body and soul unto everlasting life.' The 1552 *Book of Common Prayer* replaced these words with a form that more closely reflected the theological position of Zwingli and Calvin. All reference to the body and blood of Christ was removed: 'Take and eat this in remembrance that Christ died for thee and feed on him in thy heart by faith with thanksgiving.' 'Feed on him in thy heart' was a poetic way of forwarding the Reformed theology that taught that it is through faith alone that the grace of God is received, not through the substance of the sacrament. Cranmer's new Prayer Book was teaching the belief that Christ was to be received in the heart, not in the hand.

The Peace was removed.

The Lord's Prayer changed places, and instead of immediately following the consecration it was to be said after receiving communion (thereby placing the emphasis on the receiver and not on what is received).

The *Agnus Dei* ('O Lamb of God') was also removed, so too was the *Benedictus* ('Blessed is he that cometh in the name of the Lord') earlier in the service.

The Prayer of Oblation, which had formed the second part of the consecration prayer in 1549, was separated and placed at the end of the service as one of two Post Communion Prayers.

The *Gloria* was placed at the very end of the service before the General Blessing.

Not far enough

Cranmer was willing to strip out of his first Prayer Book much of the ceremonial as well as much of the traditional Catholic doctrine. However, he still retained some of the features and phrases that many of his most radical colleagues wished he had eliminated. For example, 'priest' continued to be used alongside 'minister', and kneeling to receive the sacrament endured despite protests from John Knox, among others, who argued that Communion should always be received seated.

So loud was the call from certain quarters for the 1552 *Book of Common Prayer* to go further than its author was proposing, that there was a delay in publication by a fortnight as pressure was applied on the Archbishop by members of the Regency Council. They urged him to reconsider the rubric on kneeling to receive Communion. Cranmer refused to give way so a compromise was found. The rubric stating that people should receive Communion 'in their hands kneeling' was retained, but an additional rubric was added at the end of the service that reflected the opinions of Cranmer's more radical colleagues. It was called the Black Rubric.

The Black Rubric

The Black Rubric was a doctrinal statement that explicitly rejected the real presence of Christ in the Eucharist. It neatly summed up the Protestant doctrine that many had been pushing the second Prayer Book to enshrine.

Although no order can be so perfectly devised, but it may be of some, either for their ignorance and infirmity, or else of malice and obstinacy, misconstrued, depraved, and interpreted in a wrong part: and yet because brotherly charity willeth, that so much as conveniently may be, offences should be taken away: therefore we are willing to do the same. Whereas it is ordained in the *Book of Common Prayer*, in the administration of the Lord's Supper that the communicants kneeling should receive the Holy Communion: which thing being well meant, for a signification of the humble and grateful acknowledging of the benefits of Christ, given unto the worthy receiver, and to avoid the profanation and disorder, which about the Holy Communion might else ensue: lest yet the same kneeling might be thought or taken otherwise, we do declare that it is not meant thereby that any adoration is done, or ought to be done, either unto the Sacramental bread or wine there bodily received, or unto any real and essential presence there being of Christ's natural flesh and blood. For as concerning the Sacramental bread and wine, they remain still in their very natural substances, and therefore may not be adored, for that were idolatry to be abhorred by all faithful Christians and as concerning the natural body and blood of our Saviour Christ, they are in heaven and not here. For it is against the truth of Christ's natural true body to be in more places than in one at one time.

Baptism

Cranmer simplified this service still further, removing several elements of the 1549 service. Signing with the sign of the cross at the beginning was removed, as were the exorcisms. The Lord's Prayer and the Creed were also dropped. The prayer said by the priest was now to be said by the congregation. A short collect replaced the blessing of the water. The signing of the cross after Baptism was retained but the giving of the robe of baptism was stripped from the service.

Confirmation

This short rite became shorter with the removal of the making of the sign of the cross and the specific form of words that accompanied it. No collects or readings were provided for the celebration of Communion at confirmation.

Holy Matrimony

The most significant change in the second Prayer Book was the removal of 'the tokens of spousage'. The continued use of the wedding ring in the 1552 book came as a great disappointment to the radicals who wanted to see the removal of all symbols from the *Book of Common Prayer*.

Visitation of the Sick

The service was shortened and anointing removed. The Confession and Absolution, against strong opposition, was retained, but all mention to the possible use of Confession and Absolution at other times was removed.

Communion of the Sick

This service was retained, perhaps surprisingly. The *Kyries* were removed and no provision was made for the saying or singing of the *Gloria*. It is unclear whether the materials in this service were provided for the celebration of Communion in the sick person's home or not. The rubric only directs the priest to 'minister the Holy Communion'.

Burial

Again, this service was significantly reduced and no option was given for a service in church, only at the graveside. Similarly, no liturgical provision was made for Communion, implying that it should no longer play a part in the ceremonies of Burial.

The longest part of this shortened Burial service was the Bible reading from 1 Corinthians 15. All other readings, including the provision of Psalms, were removed.

The choice of the Bible reading is significant for what it tells us about the theological shift taking place. The final collect in the 1552 *Book of Common Prayer* Burial service lays particular stress upon the hope of resurrection. When understood in the light of the preceding collect (with its stress on the accomplishment of 'the number of thine elect') it teaches the theology of the salvation of the elect. For this reason – that only the elect are saved – there is no commendation for the departed because none should be necessary (or in the case of one preordained to damnation, a commendation would be pointless).

The Churching of Women

This service was given a new name. In the 1549 book it had been the 'Purification of Women' but in 1552 *Book of Common Prayer* it was called 'The Thanksgiving of Women after Childbirth, commonly called the Churching of Women'.

This short service remains largely unchanged. The beginning rubric, like that at Morning Prayer, changed the location of the service from 'nigh unto the choir door' to 'nigh unto the place where the table standeth', that is, it moved away from the medieval sanctuary into the Reformation chancel or nave. The final rubric, in keeping with the removal of the robe of baptism from the Baptism service, removes the requirement for the woman at her 'churching' to offer her 'crysome'. In 1552, only the 'accustomed offerings' are required, and it is still envisaged that the mother received Communion following, but only 'if convenient'.

Commination against Sinners

No changes in the content of this service were made as the service in the 1549 book was very much in the best spirit of the Reformation. But this service did receive a change of name. It was called the 'Commination against Sinners' from the Latin *comminari* – to threaten.

The short life of the second *Book of Common Prayer* (1552)

Only months after the publication of the 1552 *Book of Common Prayer* and in order to reinforce the Protestant character of its doctrine, the Forty-Two Articles were published. Though the bishops had not been consulted, the articles claimed the authority of 'the bishops and other learned men in the Synod at London in the year of our Lord God 1552', and they carried a royal mandate. This was Cranmer's work, and he composed it in 1552 at about the time that he and others were revising the liturgy. The articles strongly reinforced reformed doctrines that had been so successfully enshrined in the new service book. A royal mandate from June 1553 required that they were to be taught throughout the Church and subscribed to by all clergy, graduates and other office holders.

However, time did not allow the articles of June 1553 nor the *Book of Common Prayer* of the previous year to take hold. A young king was dying and those around him, most particularly the Lord Protector (the newly ennobled Duke of Northumberland), felt that power was passing from them.

On 6 July 1553, shortly after the Forty-Two Articles had been published, Edward VI died and Edward's half-sister Mary was proclaimed Queen, though not at first as Edward's will had excluded Mary from the succession in favour of his cousin Lady Jane Grey. Attempts to fix the succession failed. A Catholic now acceded to a Protestant Throne.

Those with power during Edward's reign had sought to make England Protestant. In Edward's name two Prayer Books had been published with the authority of Parliament and claiming the authority of the Church, the second book more radical than the first. But neither of these books, nor any Act of Parliament, would ever be as effective in making the English people Protestant as the accession of Mary I.

Mary and the abolition of the *Book of Common Prayer*

The *Book of Common Prayer* died with Edward. On Mary's accession, which Lord Protector Northumberland and his fellow members of the Privy Council had tried desperately to prevent, the 'Old Religion' was restored at once. The tide quickly turned against the Reformation, and a number of the leading Reformers of the day took flight and set sail for the Continent, fearing for the backlash that would come. Cranmer's friend Peter Martyr was among them. Cranmer remained.

Mary began work immediately to restore England to Rome by restoring the Latin Mass. At her coronation in 1553, Mary swore an oath of loyalty to the Pope. This was more theoretical than practical. The Royal Supremacy established by her father could not be easily unpicked. The new liturgy of the Church of England, however, could.

The Acts of Parliament passed under Edward enforcing the use of the *Book of Common Prayer* were immediately repealed. Clerical celibacy was re-enforced, and Thomas Cranmer, author of the prayers of the English Reformation, was removed from office and placed behind bars. He was not alone: Hooper, Coverdale, Latimer and Ridley were all deposed.

Reginald Pole, the papal legate, set sail and arrived in England, and in front of him 500 members of Parliament knelt to confess their errors and to receive his absolution. Acts of Parliament against the Pope's authority were removed from the statute book, and both Parliament and the Church affirmed their faith in the doctrine of Transubstantiation – a central question and controversy of the Reformation. Mary put the Mass back into Latin and restored the Sarum Use.

Less than two years after her accession Mary commanded, on 4 February 1555, that the first fires should be kindled at Smithfield to punish those who refused to repent of their schism and heresy. Those fires soon spread to Oxford where, after his trial in the University Church, Thomas Cranmer stood condemned of heresy. The story of Thomas Cranmer's trial and death – his sudden recantation and then his even more sudden

retraction – is now the stuff of legend. The hand that worked
to compose and translate the first and second English Prayer
Book was the same hand that had denied its doctrine by signing the recantation. It was the hand that Cranmer held up to
the flames first.

The third *Book of Common Prayer* (1559)

The Catholic restoration that Mary committed herself to would
only ever survive if she could produce an heir. Rumours that
she had conceived a child with her husband Philip of Spain
spread throughout the court and the country in 1555, but her
pregnancy was a phantom. Mary died on 17 November 1558.
A few hours later the Archbishop of Canterbury, Reginald
Pole, also died. With them died the dream of restoring England
to the Papacy.

Mary was succeeded by her half-sister, Elizabeth, who was
always going to be committed to the reforms of the Church of
England because of her mother and her upbringing. She was
the daughter of Anne Boleyn, a convinced Protestant and to
many a heroine of the Protestant cause, and Elizabeth had been
raised and schooled in the Reformed tradition. But the content
of her Protestantism (was it radical, moderate or conservative?)
was unknown. Would she be more like her half-brother and
promote further reform in liturgy, doctrine and Church order,
or more conservative like her father and look to establish a
non-Roman Catholicism?

What is clear is that the centrepiece to Elizabeth's religious
policy for settling her kingdom was a Prayer Book that would
appeal to both factions.

This wouldn't be easy to accomplish. Mary had greatly
influenced the choice of the bishops and others whose support
was essential if Elizabeth was to achieve the settlement she
sought. Yet after considerable debate, manoeuvring and not
a little scheming, the 1559 Act of Supremacy passed through
Parliament.

Elizabeth's Act of Supremacy

The Act was the second of its kind (the first passed in 1534 under Henry and had been abolished 20 years later by Mary), but Elizabeth was more carefully moderate than her father in asserting her authority over the Church. Knowing full well that the stability of a highly unstable kingdom could only be achieved if there was a large degree of peace in the Church, Elizabeth worked to appease Protestants and Catholics alike. Elizabeth's Act of Supremacy jettisoned the title 'Supreme Head' to describe her jurisdiction over the Church. Many Catholics had protested at this and some had sacrificed their lives in protest. Elizabeth knew this and so she chose instead the more nuanced 'Supreme Governor'. Perhaps this revealed the Queen's more conservative religious feelings, or it may have been a necessary and canny decision to secure a wide base of support in the country. Whatever the motives, it is the title that the monarch still bears today.

And if Catholic concerns were addressed by Elizabeth, so too were Protestant sensibilities. The new Act of Supremacy restated the claim of the English Crown over 'the state ecclesiastical and spiritual . . . abolishing all foreign power [Pope] repugnant to the same'.

The other thing that the Act of Supremacy enforced was the Oath of Supremacy. This required anyone holding public office in the State or the Church to 'declare in their conscience that the Queen's highness is the only supreme governor of this realm . . . as well as in spiritual or ecclesiastical'. To hold office in the Elizabethan State you had to reject the power of 'any foreign prelate'.

This legislation was passed with considerable difficulty in 1559. At least nine bishops voted against it, but crucially it was accompanied not only by an Oath but by a Book. Under the terms of the 1559 Act of Uniformity it was a criminal offence not to attend church each week, and while at church it was an offence not to use the new *Book of Common Prayer*.

The 1559 Elizabethan Prayer Book was not really new at all. It was the short-lived book of 1552 with certain subtle yet significant changes.

Morning and Evening Prayer

The rubric stating where these services should take place was amended so that the services should be said 'in the accustomed place', that is in the place where the 1549 *Book of Common Prayer* had placed them (near the altar).

The issue of what the priest should wear – a constant theme of controversy throughout the Elizabethan period – was addressed with new guidance. The 1552 *Book of Common Prayer* had stipulated that only the surplice should be worn, but the 1559 revision adopted the Ornaments Rubric of 1549 and so allowed the use of a wider variety of vestments, including the cope and 'vestment' (chasuble).

Holy Communion

In the Communion, the ordering of prayers remained the same as in 1552, but the words of administration were changed. These had been radically altered in the 1552 *Book of Common Prayer* to reflect a theology that placed the emphasis on the worthiness of the receiver. In the 1559 *Book of Common Prayer*, the words of 1552 were kept but the words of 1549 were revived, and they were more catholic in tone and teaching.

1549
The body/blood of our Lord Jesus Christ which was given/ shed for thee, preserve thy body and soul unto everlasting life.

1552
Take and eat this in remembrance that Christ died for thee, and feed on him in thy heart by faith, with thanksgiving.

Drink this in remembrance that Christ's blood was shed for thee, and be thankful.

1559

The body of our Lord Jesus Christ which was given for thee, preserve thy body and soul unto everlasting life. Take and eat this in remembrance that Christ died for thee and feed on him in thy heart by faith, with thanksgiving.

The blood of our Lord Jesus Christ which was given for thee, preserve thy body and soul unto everlasting life. Drink this in remembrance that Christ's blood was shed for thee, and be thankful.

The eucharistic doctrine of the new *Book of Common Prayer* was of fundamental importance to those who, like Matthew Parker, Elizabeth's new Archbishop, consciously worked to cultivate compromise and a middle way ('via media') in the Church. The 1559 formula of words for the administration of Communion was intended to embrace those who did and those who did not believe in the real presence of Christ in the Eucharist. Men and women with Catholic and Protestant convictions alike could find something in these words to express their faith. Significantly, the Black Rubric was removed.

The Litany

The Prayer for the Queen's Majesty – now familiar to us because of its inclusion among the State Prayers in the 1662 *Book of Common Prayer* – was composed and added to the Litany alongside the new prayer 'for the Clergy and People'. In Cranmer's original 1549 Litany (based on his 1544 version), the Pope had been condemned and denounced in a memorable phrase: 'From all sedition & privy conspiracy, from the tyranny of the Bishop of Rome and all his detestable enormities, from all false doctrine . . . Good Lord, deliver us.' It says a great deal about the serious attempts being made to settle the

Church and pacify the kingdom (as well as to foster good diplomatic relations abroad) that this denunciation was removed from the 1559 *Book of Common Prayer* despite the heated polemics of this period.

One year after it was authorized, the Elizabethan Prayer Book was published in Latin (1560) for use in the Universities of Oxford and Cambridge where undergraduates were taught in Latin. Called the *Liber Precum Publicarum*, it was not in the strictest sense a true translation of the 1559 *Book of Common Prayer* that had recently passed through Parliament. In fact it resembled the more catholic 1549 liturgy, but it was short-lived and was retranslated in 1571 and made more like its English equivalent. That didn't stop many from thinking that the Queen was willing for it to have been published, because it reflected her own more catholic liturgical tastes. After all, she ensured that a crucifix was retained in the Chapel Royal and she gave short shrift to the wife of her Archbishop, which suggested to some that Elizabeth had little sympathy with the idea of a married clergy.

Yet in 1559 Elizabeth had dismissed monks with tapers at Westminster Abbey with the assurance that she could see very well without the aid of their candles, and a year earlier she commanded the Bishop of Carlisle not to elevate the host at Communion in the Chapel Royal, a command that he refused to obey and that led to the Queen leaving after the Gospel reading. The Queen's religious convictions were deliberately hard to read.

The fourth *Book of Common Prayer* (1604)

James I and VI

The reign of the Virgin Queen ended on 24 March 1603, and with Elizabeth died the House of Tudor. She had reigned for 46 years, and during that time she had by a mixture of good judgement and good luck avoided the painful upheavals and conflicts of previous reigns. In so doing Elizabeth had become a Protestant heroine to her people. Elizabeth's excommunication in 1571 by Pius V only served to make her a symbol of Protestant national resistance against Catholic Europe. It was during her reign that the *Book of Common Prayer* became deeply rooted in the lives, spirituality and imagination of the English.

The Virgin Queen died without an heir. Elizabeth's vacant throne was filled by her cousin James VI of Scotland, who ruled over a kingdom where the Protestant Reformation was most firmly established. James's accession kindled hope in those whose hopes of further liturgical reform during Elizabeth's reign had been frustrated. The Queen had defiantly refused to alter any part of the *Book of Common Prayer*. Their time had come, they felt. After all, James was a member of the Kirk, a Church that was governed not by bishops but along Presbyterian lines. The Kirk had a service book – the *Book of Common Order* – that much more closely resembled the service books of Geneva and Zurich and was admired by Reformers in England.

The Millenary Petition

As James headed south to his new capital and his new throne, he was presented with a petition. It was called the Millenary Petition (so called because it claimed the signatures of 1,000 clergymen of the Church of England). These people had been exasperated at the ways that Elizabeth had blocked the changes they proposed to the 1559 Prayer Book. These complaints they now brought to James who, they believed, would listen with a sympathetic ear.

Their key concerns were the 'popish dregs' they believed the Prayer Book retained and that they wanted abolished. The petitioners pleaded with James to free them from their 'common burden of human rites and ceremonies'.

James's response was to summon a conference at Hampton Court that met in January 1604. To it he invited representatives of the clergy who had signed the petition as well as leading bishops. James loved argument and dispute, and he fancied himself as a skilled debater. So the King himself presided over the conference, chairing its meetings and testing the arguments of those attending. England's new scholar-king relished the occasion.

The petitioners (traditionally called Puritans) argued that the reform of the liturgy in 1552 had not gone far enough. Certain 'wicked men', it was said, had prevented Thomas Cranmer from making the 1552 book a perfect liturgy. The 1559 *Book of Common Prayer* had been a backward step, they felt.

Their specific objections to the 1559 *Book of Common Prayer* were:

- The continued use of the signing with the sign of the cross at baptism.
- Confirmation, which they wanted abolished.
- The Ornaments Rubric, which was too catholic because it permitted eucharistic vestments.
- The ring in marriage – Puritans were suspicious of symbols and other material objects used in worship because of their fear of 'idolatry'.
- The length of services – they wanted shorter liturgies to allow for longer sermons.
- Bowing at the name of Jesus.
- Reading from the Apocrypha in the table of lessons.

The petitioners proved themselves canny in what they asked for and in what they didn't: they didn't include on their list the abolition of Church government by bishops (episcopacy), which was their chief ambition. This was because James, even though he was from a Presbyterian Church, was committed to episcopacy and had even tried to introduce episcopacy into the Scottish Kirk as early at 1600.

The Hampton Court Conference (1604)

To Hampton Court the new King summoned eight bishops and a handful of leading Puritans. The Puritans were led by John Rainholds, a scholar of Greek, Dean of Lincoln and a committed Calvinist, who was born in the year the first Prayer Book was published. Across the table from the Puritans sat the bishops, led by the Archbishop of Canterbury, John Whitgift, and Richard Bancroft (who became Archbishop only two months later after Whitgift's death). Over three days a range of matters was discussed, and on certain issues, like Church discipline, there was compromise and agreement. On liturgical matters, however, the bishops were less willing to compromise. James too was less than sympathetic to Puritan demands. He wrote in his diary: 'we have kept such a revel with the Puritans here these last two days . . . they fled me so from argument to argument'.

The result of the meeting disappointed the Puritans and bolstered the bishops. The surplice was to be retained and the wedding ring kept. Services were to remain 'longsome', as the Puritans called it. The word 'priest' was to be retained alongside 'minister'.

However, there were some points where agreement was reached. The absolution at Morning and Evening Prayer was also to be called 'the remission of sins', because the Puritans disliked the Catholic overtones of the word 'absolution'. Confirmation would also be called 'or the laying on of hands' for the same reason. In the Marriage service, 'with my body I thee worship' was changed to 'with my body I thee honour', which addressed Puritan sensitivities that 'the words of marriage were to be made more clear'. Lessons from the Apocrypha were reduced in number. In addition, another royal prayer was added to the Litany, this time for the Royal Family.

The *Book of Common Prayer* of 1604 appeared in print less than a month after this gathering, but it was not the book most associate with the conference. The delegates all agreed with John Rainholds when he asked the King 'to direct that the Bible be now translated, such versions as are extant not answering to the original'. The King agreed, commenting on how he disliked the Geneva Bible most of all. The King's agreement set in train the work of translation that led to the King James Version of the Bible, published seven years after the conference in 1611.

The Prayer Book north of the Border

James held a firm belief – 'No Bishop, No King'. His firm commitment to episcopacy had led him as early as 1600 to introduce bishops into the Scottish Kirk. The Kirk expressed its opposition to the idea, but the King was persistent and in 1610 ensured that three bishops were consecrated and established under the Articles of Perth (1618). These articles also established a number of liturgical canons (Church laws relating to worship) such as kneeling at Communion. James's Scottish bishops soon began work to reform the very reformed liturgy of the Scottish Church in order to bring it more into line with the use in England. For them, the Prayer Book was the model to follow, but the bishops were too zealous and too far out of sympathy with the Protestant Church in which they ministered. The book they eventually produced – the 1637 Scottish Liturgy – caused immediate popular protest and violent reaction.

Bishop Wedderburn of Edinburgh and Archbishop Spottiswoode of Glasgow were Laudians, admirers of William Laud, Charles I's Archbishop of Canterbury, and his more Catholic liturgical tastes and theology. These Scottish bishops were inspired by the revival they saw going on south of the border, a revival of liturgical customs that to many in the wider population appeared too similar to the customs of the pre-Reformation Church. Wedderburn and Spottiswoode admired the 1549 *Book of Common Prayer* most of all. They saw in it a liturgy that was closer to the medieval services than later Prayer Books had been, and attempted to compose a Scottish Liturgy that more closely resembled the 1549 *Book of Common Prayer*. In so doing these men opened a wound that would not heal.

The 1637 Scottish *Book of Common Prayer* had been their passion and their project, but it soon became known as 'Laud's Book', a name that expressed the fear and anger of many in Scotland that the English Church and English *Book of Common Prayer* were being imposed on the Scottish people. Suspicions were high and war was near.

The Civil War and the abolition of the Book of Common Prayer

War was not caused by a liturgy alone, however ill-judged its implementation may have been. The English Civil War, like all wars between neighbours, was vicious, bitter, and the culmination of many different factors. The *Book of Common Prayer* was just one of them. Opponents of the liturgical reforms of the 1630s in Scotland made common cause with those in England whose hopes for reforming the Church had been frustrated by Elizabeth and James, and who in Charles saw a firm opponent of the doctrinal and liturgical standards and system that they hoped to establish.

Driven by a determination to defend the Reformation in Scotland and to further the cause of Reformation in England, radical Protestants north of the border joined forces with their English sympathizers and formed the Solemn League and Covenant, which was officially signed in 1643, shortly after the beginning of the war. This covenant was the amalgamation of a number of campaigning movements for radical liturgical change.

The Solemn League and Covenant

From among the list of their demands, two stand out:

- 'We shall sincerely, really and constantly . . . endeavour . . . the Reformation of religion in England in doctrine, worship, discipline and government, according to the word of God and the example of the best reformed churches.' This meant the services of the churches across the Channel, the liturgies of which had inspired the Kirk's own *Book of Common Order*.
- 'We, in like manner, endeavour the extirpation of popery & prelacy'. Episcopal Church government was their target, and any religious practice that continued a practice that they identified with Catholicism. The covenanters had come to hate bishops.

The covenanters were clear: the *Book of Common Prayer* must be changed, and by force of arms if necessary. So too must the way the Church was ordered under bishops. Mindful of his father's words 'No Bishop, No King', the demands of the covenanters must have been heard by Charles I with foreboding.

It was only later in the Civil War that the covenanters achieved their goals, but achieve them they did. On 3 January 1645, 96 years after its use was first enforced by Parliament, an Ordinance of Parliament formally abolished the *Book of Common Prayer* and replaced it with the *Directory of Public Worship*. The *Directory* was a manual that offered the user a series of directions about how public worship should be conducted. It included very few authorized prayers and no formal rites as the *Book of Common Prayer* did. It was a very different kind of book.

The *Book of Common Prayer* had been abolished because, as one of the many protestors at the time put it, 'it is a liturgy, for the most part, framed out of the Romish Breviary, Rituals [and] Mass book'. The Puritans rejected anything that had its roots from before the Reformation. But the Puritans were now in the ascendency. A further law was passed by the Long Parliament (so called because it sat for eight years from 1640 to 1648) outlawing the use of the *Book of Common Prayer*. On 23 August 1645, it became illegal to use the Prayer Book in any 'public place of worship or in any private place or family'. A rising scale of fines was imposed on those who dared to break the law, with 'one whole year's imprisonment without bail or mainprize' for those caught for a third offence.

The *Directory of Public Worship* on the other hand (known as the *Westminster Directory* in Scotland) followed the liturgical principles set out in Geneva and satisfied the opponents of the *Book of Common Prayer*. John Knox was its Thomas Cranmer.

The irony in this series of events is that the Scottish bishops with the support of the King had hoped to establish liturgical uniformity across the two kingdoms by the introduction of the

Book of Common Prayer north of the border. The reaction to this, however, was the abolition of the liturgical system they most admired and the establishment of a liturgy they most opposed. In fact, so complete was the rejection of the *Book of Common Prayer* in the aftermath of civil war that revenge was not only taken against the Prayer Book but against the Church whose doctrine and order was defined by that liturgy. The Church of England ceased to be and it too was abolished.

The same day the *Book of Common Prayer* was made illegal, William Laud the Archbishop of Canterbury was stripped of all titles and condemned to death. The following year episcopacy itself was abolished. 'No Bishop, No King', James I had stated. Charles I was beheaded on the morning of 30 January 1649.

The best we have seen: Interregnum and Restoration

Between 1645 and 1660, the Church of England and the *Book of Common Prayer* did not legally exist. Both had been reformed out of existence. In their place was the Commonwealth ruled over by Oliver Cromwell, the Lord Protector. Yet by the death of Oliver Cromwell in September 1658, it was clear to many that the Protectorate he had established, as much by the force of his own personality, could not outlive him. No sooner had his son Richard succeeded as Lord Protector than he stepped down.

Parliament began to look across the Channel to where the future Charles II was in exile. They sent a band of parliamentarians and Presbyterians to bring the King back. The Presbyterian leaders who sailed to The Hague asked the King if he would forsake the Prayer Book, which had been discontinued. They also presented to Charles their well-rehearsed concerns and complaints about the *Book of Common Prayer*. Charles was canny. He knew that he had yet to be crowned and proclaimed King on English soil, so he therefore, on 1 May 1660, gave the Presbyterians some assurance that their views would be heard by issuing the Declaration of Breda. The declaration promised toleration of the religious differences that had torn England apart during the Civil War, and three days later he received the Presbyterians and heard their concerns. On 10 May 1660, the House of Lords, when gathering to worship, used the 1604 Prayer Book once again for the first time in 15 years.

A National Synod

On 25 October 1660, the King issued a statement on the liturgy in reply to the petitions he had received at The Hague asking him to resist restoring the Prayer Book. The *Book of Common Prayer* was 'the best we have seen', the King said. However, Charles II appreciated the need to build peace in a divided kingdom and so he called 'a national Synod' to address the issues of the Prayer Book. His hope was that if agreement could finally be achieved on the *Book of Common Prayer*, England could be settled again.

Five months later, on Lady Day, 25 March 1661, Charles called a conference that met on 15 April and ran through to 24 July. The delegates assembled at the old Palace of the Savoy, just off the Strand, on the site where a hotel and a theatre of the same name now stand. It was this Savoy Conference and its decisions that would shape the *Book of Common Prayer* that we have and use today.

Delegates came from two very different camps – Puritan and episcopal. The former represented the 'godly', those who had campaigned hard for a radical form of Protestantism and who, under the Protectorate of Cromwell, had been very much in the driving seat. The episcopal bench opposite them represented the existing bishops whose ministry had been abruptly – and in some cases violently – ended during the preceding years of the Commonwealth. They were on the rise again. Puritan and episcopal delegates met across the table at the Savoy. It was not an easy meeting.

Each side had 12 men with a further nine in attendance. The Savoy Conference resembled the conference at Hampton Court some 56 years earlier. As then, the Puritans were led by a Reynolds, this time Edward Reynolds, Bishop of Norwich. Alongside him were leading Presbyterians such as Richard Baxter (poet, hymn-writer and 'the chief of English Protestant Schoolmen') and John Lightfoot, an eminent biblical scholar.

Across the table sat the bishops, who were in no mood to compromise. They were led by the Archbishop of York (who rejoiced in the name Accepted Frewen), but the episcopal bench was in reality led by Gilbert Sheldon, Bishop of London, who later became Archbishop of Canterbury. He was joined by John Cosin among others. Cosin was a noted liturgist, Bishop of Durham, and a man of Catholic convictions.

It is hard for us, standing at such a distance from these events, to appreciate how emotionally and politically charged this encounter must have been. The execution of the King in 1649 had left an indelible mark on England, and especially on the bishops who had defended Charles and the Church of England. In addition, the banning of traditional worship and practice, and the active persecution of Anglicans in the late 1640s and throughout the 1650s, had created enormous resentment towards the Puritan group on the part of the bishops. Small wonder the bishops had little time for the 'Exceptions' to the Prayer Book that the Puritans were about to list.

Much like Hampton Court, the Savoy Conference got under way with the bishops stating that they were content with the liturgy and doctrine of the 1604 *Book of Common Prayer*. They invited the Puritan representatives to list their 'Exceptions' to the liturgy. The Puritans willingly obliged. Among their grievances they included greater liberty for the minister to withhold absolution and 'to admit and to keep' from the Lord's Table. They demanded the removal of 'Lord have mercy upon us and incline our hearts . . .' from after each of the Ten Commandments, believing that 'the people's part in public prayer to be only with silence and reverence . . . and to declare their consent in the close, by saying "Amen"'. Collects should also be abolished and edited into 'one methodical and entire form of prayer'. The Litany should become a single long prayer. The Ornaments Rubric – directing what the clergy should wear – should be removed, kneeling at Communion should be suppressed, and making the sign of the cross at Baptism should be abolished once and for all. The wedding ring must be made optional, and all references to Lent and to saints' days should be removed.

The Baptism service should be changed to drop any reference to the baptized person being 'regenerate'. Baptism should only be administered by a minister, even in an emergency (to stop the practice of midwives baptizing dying children at birth). The Burial of the Dead should omit any reference to the resurrection of the dead person (because that would have assumed, from a Puritan point of view, that the dead person was one of the elect when they might not be). Confirmation should not be administered by bishops exclusively.

The 'Exceptions' was a tactical mistake. Although their objections to the *Book of Common Prayer* were numerous and argued at length, the Puritans brought nothing new to the Savoy. They rehearsed old arguments about the errors of the *Book of Common Prayer*, most of which had been stated in the Millenary Petition of 1603. This meant that the bishops, who were already in no mood to indulge the process any longer than they had to, were even less likely to listen.

In their reply to the 'Exceptions', the bishops robustly defended the theology, liturgy and ceremonies of the *Book of Common Prayer*: 'It was the wisdom of our Reformers to draw up such a Liturgy as neither Romanist nor Protestant could justly except against . . . For preserving of the Church's peace we know no better nor efficacious way than our set Liturgy.'

Yet perhaps surprisingly, even though there was little sympathy around the table for the other's position, the Savoy delegates did find certain points of agreement and even compromise. It was agreed that the Epistles and Gospels for Communion were to come from the King James Version, with the Epistles to be introduced more clearly by a new rubric, and the manual acts were added to the Prayer of Consecration. These directed the priest at certain points of the consecration to 'take the Paten into his hands . . . and here to break the Bread . . . and here to lay his hand upon all the Bread . . . here he is to take the

Cup into his hand . . . and here to lay his hand upon every vessel (be it Chalice of Flagon) in which there is any Wine to be consecrated'.

The Catechism was altered, in a subtle but significant way, to reflect a stronger theology of the sacramental. The Puritans reluctantly agreed to the insertion of 'as generally necessary to salvation' into the statement that there were two sacraments ordained by Christ in his Church. The bishops wanted a recognition that other 'institutions' in the Church such as marriage and ordination could also be considered sacraments. 'Til death us depart' in the Marriage service was altered to 'till death us do part'.

The Savoy Conference disbanded on 24 July 1661. It had succeeded in affirming the mutual antipathy between episcopal and Presbyterian parties in the Church, but it had also established the broad parameters within which the new *Book of Common Prayer* would be revised and taken through Parliament. Sufficient consultation, more than the bishops at least felt was necessary, had been made from among those who had the strongest objections to the liturgy.

Convocation met in November 1661 to discuss and revise the Prayer Book. The job was done at speed. In fact the entire process was completed within a month, with much of the discussions centring not on the liturgical texts themselves but on the rubrics. The wording of some rubrics had been agreed in the summer at the Savoy, but that of others had not, such as the rubrics at Holy Communion. During the revision process these came to affirm more explicitly a theology of the real presence of Christ in the Eucharist by the frequent use of the language of 'consecration'. For example, such directions as 'The Priest . . . shall say the Prayer of Consecration, as followeth' and 'If the consecrated Bread or Wine be all spent before all have communicated, the Priest is to consecrate more', were inserted into the Holy Communion along with reference to 'consecrated Elements'. Largely left to three Bishops – Cosin of Durham, Sanderson of Lincoln and Wren of Ely – the work of revising the *Book of Common Prayer* pushed forward at pace. To the new *Book of Common Prayer* some new services were also added: a rite for baptizing adults and a form of service to be used at sea. The new Baptism service was a practical and pastoral response to the reality that many adults in England had not been baptized because of the popular rejection of Baptism – especially infant Baptism – by most of the religious sects and groups that proliferated in the 1640s and 1650s. In addition, the bishops saw a need for a service of adult baptism that met the needs of missionaries in Maryland, Virginia, and elsewhere along the coastline of North America.

The form of prayer to be used at sea similarly recognized a new situation of increased trade and traffic across the oceans with these emerging markets.

Additional prayers were also added to the new Prayer Book by request, most significantly the General Thanksgiving, composed by Edward Reynolds who had led the Puritans at Savoy, a prayer that has become a classic liturgical text of Anglicanism.

Four days before Christmas in 1661, the fifth and final *Book of Common Prayer* was completed and adopted by Convocation. Early the following year, it moved to Westminster and passed through Parliament. The 1662 *Book of Common Prayer* became the legal service book of the Church once the Act of Uniformity passed through the House of Lords on 9 April 1662 and had received the assent of Charles II on 19 May that year.

St Bartholomew's day was appointed for its introduction into the Church – 24 August – when 'all incumbents of England, under penalties of losing their Livings' were to use it. Many incumbents felt they could not and left the Church of England. Richard Baxter was one of them, and along with as many as 2,500 others, Baxter left the Church of England on grounds of conscience. He could no longer subscribe to the doctrine of the *Book of Common Prayer* as the law demanded. These ministers established the Free Churches and became known as Nonconformists, because they could not conform to the 1662 Act of Uniformity and the Prayer Book it established.

A *mean betwixt two extremes*

As Thomas Cranmer had written a Preface to the 1549 *Book of Common Prayer* to explain the thinking behind it and the principles underpinning it, so too did the compilers of the 1662 *Book of Common Prayer*. Cranmer's original preface was kept and renamed 'concerning the service of the Church' because it was felt, even by 1662, to be a classic statement of Anglican liturgical principles.

The new Preface was not unlike Cranmer's original. It set out the case for moderation, 'to keep the mean betwixt two extremes'. These extremes were characterized as 'too much stiffness' and 'too much easiness', and even though the Preface is in places sharply critical of 'the licentiousness of the late times', it sets out the moderate intentions of the compilers of the 1662 *Book of Common Prayer*. Some services, it says, have been willingly altered 'in order for the better direction of them that are to officiate in any part of Divine Service' as well as 'for the more proper expressing of some words and phrases of ancient usage in terms more suitable to the language of the present times'. It also explains that other additions have been made in order to make the *Book of Common Prayer* more 'fitted to special occasions'.

But above all, the purpose of the 1662 *Book of Common Prayer*, its compilers argued, was to keep unity within the Church of England: 'We conceived most to tend to the preservation of Peace and Unity in the Church; the procuring of Reverence and exciting of Piety and Devotion in the Publick Worship of God.'

They were confident that the 1662 *Book of Common Prayer* 'doth not contain anything . . . which a godly man may not with a good conscience use'. Three hundred and fifty years later we are still using it.

PART 2

Using the *Book of Common Prayer*

2

Finding Your Way around the
Book of Common Prayer

The first thing worth pointing out is that the *Book of Common Prayer* isn't a single book. It is five books bound together in a single volume. The full name of the *Book of Common Prayer* summarizes what's between its pages:

> The *Book of Common Prayer and Administration of the Sacraments and other Rites and Ceremonies of the Church according to the Church of England* together with The Psalter or Psalms of David pointed as they are to be sung or said in churches and the Form and Manner of making ordaining and consecrating Bishops, Priests and Deacons.

Now you see why our liturgy is known more simply as the *Book of Common Prayer*! It is helpful, therefore, to know precisely what is in it in order to find your way around it.

The *Book of Common Prayer*

Strictly speaking, this is the name given to what used to be called Divine Service: Morning Prayer and Evening Prayer – the services that Cranmer condensed from the monastic daily services to form the backbone of his new service book. Divine Service also includes the Litany. The Litany is a long series of intercessions with a refrain after each petition. The Litany was intended to come immediately after Morning Prayer and before the Holy Communion on Wednesdays, Friday and Sundays.

The Administration of the Sacraments

Sacraments in the Church of England have always fired debate and disagreement: are there seven, are there two? The Prayer Book expresses a very Anglican pragmatism about this. By 'Administration of the Sacraments' the *Book of Common Prayer* means the two 'dominical sacraments' (sacraments instituted by the Lord himself): Holy Communion and Baptism. The way the Church of England has traditionally navigated its way through these historic and heated disagreements is to state that in the Gospels Jesus Christ instituted two sacraments only: Communion and Baptism. These are the two sacraments 'as generally necessary to salvation'. However, the existence of other sacraments is not denied in the *Book of Common Prayer*, but they are understood to be sacraments of a different order. That is why in the Prayer Book they come under the following heading.

Other Rites and Ceremonies of the Church according to the Church of England

'Those five commonly called sacraments' are listed in the twenty-fifth article of religion: Confirmation, Penance (the short rite of confession and priestly absolution found in the Visitation to the Sick), Orders (Ordination), Matrimony (Marriage), and extreme Unction ('Last Rites', which in the Prayer Book are found in the Visitation and Communion of the Sick).

Because of the way the Church of England has handled controversy over sacraments, these services are sometimes called the 'lesser sacraments'. In addition to these lesser sacraments, other services are grouped together under the heading 'other rites and ceremonies':

- Burial of the Dead.
- Churching of Women.
- The Commination.
- Forms of Prayer to be used at Sea.

Together with the Psalter or Psalms of David

The Psalter (Book of Psalms) is the only entire biblical book to be found in the *Book of Common Prayer*. Cranmer's intention was to provide a liturgy that would encourage people to pray daily, and as part of his attempt to establish a tradition of 'common prayer', the Psalter was provided in full. The Psalter is the name of the 150 Psalms that tradition attributes to King David, and that we still use today in worship. The Psalms are included in the Prayer Book in their translation by Miles Coverdale. They are divided up into morning and evening Psalms for each day of the month. The intention is that the whole of the Psalter would be read each month within the cycle of daily prayer that Cranmer had created.

Form and Manner of making ordaining and consecrating Bishops, Priests and Deacons

The common name of this book is the Ordinal, and it contains the ordination services of the Church of England. Technically, the Ordinal is not part of the Prayer Book but by tradition is added to it. It was first revised and reformed by Cranmer's German friend Martin Bucer and was published in 1550, and although minor changes were made at various points in its history, the service found in the 1662 *Book of Common Prayer* is Bucer's original work based on the medieval services that inspired it. Three distinct ordination services are provided in the Ordinal for the making of deacons, the ordaining of priests and the consecrating of bishops.

Prayers and Services found in the *Book of Common Prayer* but not listed on the title page

Over time, other services, prayers and liturgical texts have been incorporated into the *Book of Common Prayer* and now sit alongside the five main sections summarized above. They are:

- At Morning Prayer – *Quicunque vult* (called 'the Creed of St Athanasius').
- Prayers and Thanksgivings.
- A Catechism.
- Forms of Prayer with Thanksgiving to Almighty God ('Accession Service').
- The Articles of Religion ('Thirty-Nine Articles').
- A Table of Kindred and Affinity.

The Creed of St Athanasius

This isn't really a creed, but has traditionally been called a creed and so was included in the Prayer Book from the very first. In the *Book of Common Prayer* it is given its Latin name, '*Quicunque vult*', from its opening words, 'Whosoever wishes.' You may notice that the Prayer Book frequently uses the Latin names for Psalms and canticles. Confusingly, the name given to the section of the Prayer Book containing this creed is 'At Morning Prayer'. This is because the Creed of St Athanasius is appointed to be said at Morning Prayer instead of the Apostles' Creed on 13 days throughout the Christian year: Christmas Day, the Epiphany, St Matthias, Easter Day, Ascension Day, Whitsunday, St John the Baptist, St James, St Bartholomew, St Matthew, St Simon and St Jude, St Andrew and Trinity Sunday.

Prayers and Thanksgivings upon several occasions

The various prayers included in this section are:

- For Rain.
- For fair Weather.
- Two prayers in the time of Dearth and Famine.
- In the time of War and Tumults.
- In the time of any common Plague or Sickness.
- Two prayers in the Ember Weeks, to be said every day, for those who are to be admitted into Holy Orders.
- A Prayer that may be said after any of the former.
- A Prayer for the High Court of Parliament, to be read during their Session.
- A Collect or Prayer for all Conditions of men to be used at such times when the Litany is not appointed to be said.

The thanksgivings that follow are:

- A General Thanksgiving.
- For Rain.
- For Fair Weather.
- For Plenty.
- For Peace and Deliverance from our Enemies.
- For restoring Publick Peace at Home.
- Two prayers 'For Deliverance from the Plague, or other common Sickness'.

Not all prayers in the Prayer Book are well known, and some have not entered into the tradition of Anglican common prayer. The general quality of the prayers and thanksgivings in this section is not great, and their use today is rare. They haven't been taken to heart. However, two of them do stand out and, because of the quality of their language and their intention, have become firmly established in the Anglican tradition: the Prayer for all Conditions of Men and a General Thanksgiving.

A Collect or Prayer for all Conditions of men, to be used at such times when the Litany is not appointed to be said

O GOD, the Creator and Preserver of all mankind, we humbly beseech thee for all sorts and conditions of men; that thou wouldest be pleased to make thy ways known unto them, thy saving health unto all nations. More especially we pray for the good estate of the Catholick Church; that it may be so guided and governed by thy good Spirit, that all who profess and call themselves Christians may be led into the way of truth, and hold the faith in unity of spirit, in the bond of peace, and in righteousness of life. Finally we commend to thy fatherly goodness all those, who are any ways afflicted or distressed in mind, body, or estate [especially those for whom our prayers are desired] that it may please thee to comfort and relieve them, according to their several necessities, giving them patience under their sufferings, and a happy issue out of all their afflictions. And this we beg for Jesus Christ his sake. Amen.

A General Thanksgiving

ALMIGHTY God, Father of all mercies, we thine unworthy servants do give thee most humble and hearty thanks for all thy goodness and loving-kindness to us and to all men [particularly to those who desire now to offer up their praises and thanksgivings for thy late mercies vouchsafed unto them]. We bless thee for our creation, preservation, and all the blessings of this life; but above all for thine inestimable love in the redemption of the world by our Lord Jesus Christ, for the means of grace, and for the hope of glory. And we beseech thee, give us that due sense of all thy mercies, that our hearts may be unfeignedly thankful, and that we shew forth thy praise, not only with our lips, but in our lives; by giving up ourselves to thy service, and by walking before thee in holiness and righteousness all our days; through Jesus Christ our Lord, to whom with thee and the Holy Ghost be all honour and glory, world without end. Amen.

A Catechism

The Catechism, first composed for the 1549 Prayer Book, is 'an instruction to be learned of every person before he be brought to be confirmed by the Bishop'. Clear and simply set out, it is intended to 'catechize' (teach) a person (a child) in the essentials of the Christian faith. It does this in a question and answer format, covering the core Christian texts of the Apostles' Creed, the Ten Commandments, and the Lord's Prayer, as well as the sacraments, their number and their purpose.

It was written as an accompaniment to confirmation. That is why it is found in the *Book of Common Prayer* immediately before the confirmation service.

Forms of Prayer with Thanksgiving to Almighty God

This is known as the Accession Service and comes at the very back of the Prayer Book. It isn't really a service at all but a selection of suitable prayers, recommended readings, anthems and litanies for use 'in all Churches and Chapels within this Realm, every Year, upon the anniversary of the day of the Accession of the Reigning Sovereign'. It also includes a Collect, Epistle and Gospel for a celebration of the Communion, and the beautiful Prayer for Unity, a prayer that is a treasure of Anglican liturgy.

Prayer for Unity from the Accession Service

O GOD the Father of our Lord Jesus Christ, our only Saviour, the Prince of Peace: Give us grace seriously to lay to heart the great dangers we are in by our unhappy divisions. Take away all hatred and prejudice, and whatsoever else may hinder us from godly union and concord: that, as there is but one Body, and one Spirit, and one hope of our calling, one Lord, one faith, one baptism, one God and Father of us all; so we may henceforth be all of one heart, and of one soul, united in one holy bond of truth and peace, of faith and charity, and may with one mind and one mouth glorify thee; through Jesus Christ our Lord. Amen.

The Thirty-Nine Articles of Religion

The Prayer Book contains some material that is not liturgical. The Articles of Religion is one example. The Thirty-Nine Articles were added to the Prayer Book in 1563 'for the avoiding of diversities of opinions and for the establishing of consent touching true religion'. Compiled by Archbishop Matthew Parker, the Thirty-Nine Articles seek to define the common doctrinal ground of Anglicanism by addressing the controversies of the time. They seek to express what Parker called the 'via media' (middle way) between Calvinism and Roman Catholicism. The articles have traditionally been incorporated into the Prayer Book ever since that time, and are considered one of the 'historic formularies' of the Church of England. Ever since 1662, they have been prefixed in the *Book of Common Prayer* by a declaration written by Charles I.

The Table of Kindred and Affinity

In the days when Prayer Books were found in every pew or pocket, there were sections to which you turned if you were looking for a distraction during a long sermon! The table to find Easter Day at the very front of the *Book of Common Prayer* allows you locate the date of Easter 'from the present time till the year 2199 inclusive'. The other is the table at the very back of the Prayer Book that informs you who can and cannot marry. This is the Table of Kindred and Affinity. Among other things it tells a man that he cannot marry his wife's mother's mother, and a woman that she is forbidden from wedding her husband's mother's father.

Full list of contents

The *Book of Common Prayer* is a rather remarkable collection of books and other materials:

1 The Preface.
2 Concerning the Service of the Church.
3 Concerning Ceremonies, why some be abolished, and some retained.
4 Rules to Order the Service.
5 The Order how the Psalter is appointed to be read.
6 The Order how the rest of the Holy Scripture is appointed to be read.
7 A Table of Proper Lessons and Psalms.
8 The Calendar, with the Table of Lessons.
9 Tables and Rules for the Feasts and Fasts through the whole Year.
10 The Order for Morning and Evening Prayer – Introduction.
11 The Order for Morning Prayer.
12 The Order for Evening Prayer.
13 The Creed of St Athanasius.
14 The Litany.
15 Prayers and Thanksgivings upon several occasions.

This is a substantial section in the Prayer Book. It provides all the material you need for the Daily Offices (sometimes also called Divine Service or the Choir Offices).

16 The Collects, Epistles, and Gospels, to be used at the Ministration of the Holy Communion, throughout the Year.

This section contains a collect (prayer for the day), a passage of an Epistle and a Gospel reading for each Sunday and other feast days of the year. In 1552, many of the feast days were removed from the Prayer Book because of the mood of suspicion at the time surrounding saints and popular devotion to them. That is why the feast days that have a Collect, Epistle

and Gospel are major feasts only. The disciples and the Blessed
Virgin Mary are included. So too are St Paul and St Michael
and All Angels. The Prayer Book's provision of readings for
saints' days has often been criticized as too limited. Others feel
that its provision of materials is about right.

17 The Order for the Administration of The Lord's Supper
or Holy Communion.
18 The Ministration of Public Baptism of Infants.
19 The Ministration of Private Baptism of Children in Houses.
20 The Order of Baptism for those of Riper Years.
21 The Catechism.
22 The Order of Confirmation.
23 The Form of Solemnization of Matrimony.
24 The Order for the Visitation of the Sick.
25 The Communion of the Sick.
26 The Order for the Burial of the Dead.
27 The Thanksgiving of Women after Childbirth.
28 A Commination, or denouncing of God's anger and
judgements against Sinners.
29 The Psalter.
30 Forms of Prayer to be used at Sea.
31 The Form and Manner of Making, Ordaining, and
Consecrating of Bishops, Priests, and Deacons.
32 Forms of Prayer for the Anniversary of the day of
Accession of the Reigning Sovereign.
33 Royal Warrant.
34 Articles of Religion.
35 A Table of Kindred and Affinity.

3

O Lord, who hast safely brought us to the beginning of this day
Morning Prayer ('Matins')

The basic structure of the service

- Opening Penitential Sentence.
- Penitential Introduction (Bidding, General Confession, Absolution, Lord's Prayer).
- Opening dialogue and 'Glory be to the Father . . .'.
- *Venite* (Psalm 95).
- Psalm(s) for the Day, each one ending with 'Glory be to the Father . . .'.
- First Lesson 'taken out of the Old Testament'.
- *Te Deum Laudamus* ('We praise thee, O God') or *Benedicite* ('O all ye works of the Lord').
- Second Lesson 'taken out of the New Testament'.
- *Benedictus* ('Blessed be the Lord God of Israel') or *Jubilate Deo* ('O be joyful in the Lord, all ye lands').
- The Apostles' Creed.
- Dialogue ('The Lord be with you') followed by the *Kyries* ('Lord, have mercy upon us').
- Lord's Prayer (in the shorter form, without 'For thine be the kingdom, the power and the glory . . .').
- Another dialogue – traditionally called the Suffrages (because they are prayers for particular things).
- Collect for the Day – the collect for the Sunday of that week or, if it is a feast day, the collect appointed for the feast.

- The Second Collect 'for Peace'.
- Third Collect 'for Grace'.
- State Prayers – for The Queen's Majesty, the Royal Family, the Clergy and People, and a Prayer of St Chrysostom.
- The Grace.

The service in detail

Penitential Introduction

- Opening Penitential Sentence.
- Penitential Introduction (often called a bidding because the minister invites (bids) the congregation to make confession for their sins).
- General Confession (called 'general' because all say it together).
- The Absolution or Remission of Sins – this is when the minister (if a priest) 'pardoneth and absolveth all them that truly repent'.
- The Lord's Prayer (including 'For thine is the kingdom, the power and the glory . . .').

Do I have to use the Penitential Introduction each time I say Morning (or Evening) Prayer?

No.

In order for the Daily Offices to be working services used each day, praying them as printed is often impractical. Several sections are commonly left out. There are a number of 'permitted variations':

- Penitential Sentence can be omitted in favour of seasonal or other sentences (see below), or omitted altogether. Appropriate seasonal sentences are also available.

- The bidding is frequently left out along with the General Confession and the Absolution, all of which were imported into the *Book of Common Prayer* in 1552. However, a shortened bidding is available to be used at penitential times if you wish.
- If you do use the Penitential Introduction to either Morning or Evening Prayer (perhaps in Lent) and a priest is not present, then it is common either for the wording of the absolution to be changed from the 'you' to 'us' form, or for the Collect for the Twenty-First Sunday after Trinity to be used so that you can pray for pardon, peace and a 'quiet mind'. This Collect can be prayed by the officiating person alone or congregationally.
- The bidding, confession and absolution can very usefully be printed (if you are printing a separate Order of Service) on the inside cover and used as a form of preparation for the congregation to use privately before the service begins.

This alternative bidding is sometimes used instead of the longer one printed in the *Book of Common Prayer*

Beloved, we are come together in the presence of Almighty God and of the whole company of heaven to offer unto him through our Lord Jesus Christ our worship and praise and thanksgiving; to make confession of our sins; to pray, as well for others as for ourselves, that we may know more truly the greatness of God's love and shew forth in our lives the fruits of his grace; and to ask on behalf of all men such things as their well-being doth require.

Wherefore let us kneel in silence, and remember God's presence with us now.

The General Confession follows.

These alternative Opening Sentences can be used throughout the year, with or without the Penitential Introduction.

General
O worship the Lord in the beauty of holiness: let the whole earth stand in awe of him. *(Psalm 96.9)*

God is Spirit: and they that worship him must worship him in spirit and in truth. *(John 4.24)*

Advent
The night is far spent, and the day is at hand: let us therefore cast off the works of darkness, and let us put on the armour of light. *(Romans 13.12)*

Christmas
Behold, I bring you good tidings of great joy which shall be to all people: for unto you is born in the city of David, a Saviour, which is Christ the Lord. *(Luke 2.10, 11)*

Epiphany
From the rising of the sun even unto the going down of the same my name is great among the nations; and in every place incense is offered unto my name, and a pure offering: for my name is great among the nations, saith the Lord. *(Malachi 1.11)*

Lent
The sacrifices of God are a broken spirit: a broken and a contrite heart, O God, thou wilt not despise. *(Psalm 51.17)*

Passiontide
Is it nothing to you, all ye that pass by? Behold, and see if there be any sorrow like unto my sorrow. *(Lamentations 1.12)*

Good Friday
God commendeth his love toward us, in that, while we were yet sinners, Christ died for us. *(Romans 5.8)*

Easter Eve
Rest in the Lord and wait patiently for him; and he shall give thee thy heart's desire. *(Psalm 37.7, 4)*

Easter Day
Blessed be the God and Father of our Lord Jesus Christ, who according to his great mercy hath begotten us again unto a living hope by the resurrection of Jesus Christ from the dead. *(1 Peter 1.3)*

Ascension Day
Seeing that we have a great high priest that is passed into the heavens, Jesus the Son of God, let us come boldly unto the throne of grace, that we may obtain mercy and find grace to help in time of need. *(Hebrews 4.14, 16)*

Pentecost (Whitsunday)
The love of God hath been shed abroad in our hearts through the Holy Spirit which was given unto us. *(Romans 5.5)*

Trinity
God is love; and he that abideth in love abideth in God and God in him. *(1 John 4.16)*

Harvest
The earth is the Lord's, and the fullness thereof. *(Psalm 24.1)*

All Saints
Seeing we are compassed about with so great a cloud of witnesses, let us lay aside every weight, and the sin which doth so easily beset us, and let us run with patience the race that is set before us, looking unto Jesus, the author and perfecter of our faith. *(Hebrews 12.1, 2)*

Saints' Days
The righteous shall be had in everlasting remembrance; the memory of the just is blessed. *(Psalm 112.6; Proverbs 10.7)*

Time of Trouble
God is our hope and strength: a very present help in trouble.
(Psalm 46.1)

The Office of Morning Prayer

This is when the service actually begins. The Penitential Introduction was added in 1552 when the second *Book of Common
Prayer* was published, as an extended form of preparation for
the service itself. The introduction has been included in both
Morning and Evening Prayer ever since. However, the opening
words, 'O Lord, open thou our lips: and our mouth shall shew
forth thy praise', have traditionally marked the beginning of
the service. This opening dialogue is traditionally called a vers-
icle (a 'verse' or sentence of scripture) followed by a response.
In the case of Morning and Evening Prayer, the opening verse is
taken from Psalm 51.15. Versicles and responses are frequently
found in the *Book of Common Prayer* and in many other
Anglican liturgies too. They are also known as dialogues.

Venite

The Venite follows the opening dialogue between priest and
congregation. It's worth noting at this point that a priest is
not essential for Morning and Evening Prayer. The rubrics of
the Prayer Book interchange 'Priest' and 'Minister' quite freely,
and the whole service can be conducted by a lay person.

It's a common feature of the Prayer Book that the names of
Psalms or other canticles (a canticle is a passage of scripture that
is used in the liturgy as a hymn of praise to God) are given their
Latin names. This reflects the expectation of Cranmer and other
liturgical Reformers that the clergy of the Church of England
should be 'learned in the Latin tongue' (it was a common criticism
of uneducated clergy at the Reformation that such people were
'lack-latins'). The *Venite* is Psalm 95, and at Morning Prayer it is
used as an opening canticle. It works very well at the beginning of
the service because it says, 'Let us come before his presence with
thanksgiving: and shew ourselves glad in him with Psalms.'

The rubric (guidance notes) immediately before the *Venite* makes it clear that because the *Venite* is a Psalm, it will be said as a Psalm in the normal course of saying the Psalms. The whole Psalter is said each month in the *Book of Common Prayer*. Therefore 'on the nineteenth day of every month it is not to be read here, but in the ordinary course of the Psalms'. Therefore on the nineteenth day of the month, the *Venite* is to be left out, otherwise it will be said twice.

Do I have to say all of the *Venite* at each service?

No. The *Venite* can be shortened by omitting verses 8 to 11 (from 'Today if ye will hear his voice' to 'Unto whom I sware in my wrath'), concluding with the 'Glory be to the Father . . .'. In the Easter Season it can be omitted altogether in favour of the Easter Anthems that are found with the Collect and eucharistic readings for Easter Day.

Psalms for the Day

The rationale behind Morning and Evening Prayer is the regular reading of the scriptures and learning what they have to teach. The role of Psalms in the Prayer Book is part of that regular rhythm of scripture. At Morning and Evening Prayer each day a selection of the Psalms is read. The Prayer Book helpfully divides the Psalms into those to be read at the beginning and at the end of each day of the month. It does this very simply by starting with Psalm 1 and working through to Psalm 150. On certain days in the year, special Psalms are appointed (for feast and fast days) but otherwise, the deep pattern of reading the Psalms is a fundamental part of the way the *Book of Common Prayer* works. The Psalms are all conveniently contained in one place in the Prayer Book – the Psalter – and are clearly marked 'Morning Prayer Day 4' or 'Evening Prayer Day 21'. The system is incredibly simple and comprehensive.

It is important to remember that although the *Book of Common Prayer* lays everything out quite clearly, you still have a choice –

you can say the Psalms each day as they are given in the Prayer Book or you are at liberty to choose one of the Psalms for the day (although this means that you're not likely to pray through the entire Psalter in one month). Similarly, you are free to choose the Psalms as they are given in the *Common Worship* lectionary. The Psalms in the Prayer Book are divided up according to a 30-day cycle. In months where there are 31 days, the Psalms for day 30 should be repeated. The cycle then begins again.

After each Psalm the *Gloria Patri* is traditionally said ('Glory be to the Father . . .').

The First Lesson

Bible readings at Morning and Evening Prayer in the *Book of Common Prayer* are traditionally called Lessons because they teach us about God. Fundamental to the liturgical reforms that gave us the Prayer Book is the belief that the Bible contains 'all things necessary to salvation', and that because of its authority the Bible should be received and understood by all. That is why having both liturgy and Bible available in English ('a language understanded of the people') was such an important part of the liturgical reforms of Thomas Cranmer.

At both Morning Prayer and Evening Prayer, the Bible is given a prominent place: the canticles are from the Bible, so too are the versicles and responses between minister and congregation, and so are the readings. Like the reading of the Psalms, the Prayer Book's original lectionary (called 'Table of Lessons') is very simple and systematic. It begins at Genesis and works through to Revelation. That way the lectionary ensures that the whole Old Testament is read through once in a year and the New Testament three times each year.

There is an exception to this rule when a certain day is a feast day. When this happens, 'proper lessons' (lessons that are appropriate or particular to the theme of the day) are appointed for use. A rubric in the Prayer Book even gives advice on how the lesson is to be announced. Lessons are announced giving chapter and verse so that those who hear the Bible read aloud could themselves find and read the passage in their own Bibles. You can see how diligent Cranmer and the Reformers were in ensuring that the laity were informed and enabled to participate fully in the worship of the Church. It sometimes confuses people who are unfamiliar with the *Book of Common Prayer* that the scripture references are announced in reverse order: 'Here begineth the x verse of the x chapter of the book of x'. We are more familiar these days with Bible references being the other way around.

Many people think, perhaps understandably, that at a Prayer Book service only the King James Version can be read. This is not necessarily the case. In many places, the King James Version is used, but any authorized translation of the scriptures can be read. A popular choice for a *Book of Common Prayer* service is the Revised Standard Version, because it keeps some of the patterns of the King James Version but uses a more contemporary form of English. In most cathedrals, the NRSV (New Revised Standard Version) is used. Others prefer other translations. It's important to remember that you have a choice, so explore.

The First Canticle (Te Deum Laudamus *or* Benedicite)

Known by their Latin names, the *Te Deum* and the *Benedicite* are long, rich and vivid hymns of praise to God. The *Te Deum* in particular has been set to music many times for that reason. Though the *Te Deum* was and remains the more commonly used canticle at Morning Prayer, the *Benedicite* is no less ancient and was used as part of the morning services of the Church since very early times. Of the two, the *Benedicite* is the biblical text. It comes from the Song of the Three in the Apocrypha. It has been used more frequently in Lent and Advent, with the *Te Deum* associated with feasts and festivals.

The Second Lesson

Following the first canticle comes the second lesson from the New Testament.

The Second Canticle

The *Book of Common Prayer* provides a choice of second canticle: the *Benedictus* (Luke 1.68) or the *Jubilate Deo* (Psalm 100). However, the rubric before the second canticle recommends that the *Benedictus* should be used 'except when that shall happen to be read in the Chapter for the day, or for the Gospel on Saint John Baptist's Day'. This is to avoid duplication between the canticle and the Gospel reading on that feast day. In that instance, the suggestion is that the *Jubilate Deo* should be used instead. In comparison with the longer first canticles, the second canticles in the *Book of Common Prayer* are shorter, and unlike the first canticle both the *Jubilate Deo* and *Benedictus* end with the *Gloria Patri* ('Glory be to the Father . . .') just like the Psalms do.

Do I have to use both canticles at Morning Prayer?

No. Since 1872, it has been legal to use only one canticle at Morning Prayer. It is ideal to use both, but if you want to create a shorter form of Matins, then you can.

The Apostles' Creed

'Then shall be said or sung the Apostles' Creed.' This baptismal confession of the Christian faith is a feature of both Morning and Evening Prayer, and it is to be said congregationally. The rubric states that there are certain days when the Apostles' Creed should be replaced by the Creed of St Athanasius.

The Lesser Litany

This short section of dialogues between minister and congregation is often called the Lesser Litany. It leads into the Lord's Prayer in the shorter form (without 'For thine be the kingdom . . .'). That in turn leads to the dialogues of prayer called the suffrages. If you are in a parish that has a choir, then these responses can be sung, because they have been set to music by many different Anglican composers.

Collects

The prayers continue with the Collect for the Day. This collect is the one appointed for the particular Sunday or feast day it happens to be. The collects for Sundays and other special days are all to be found together in one section part-way through the *Book of Common Prayer*. The Collect for the Day is always followed by two very well-known and well-loved prayers, for Peace and for Grace.

Throughout the year only three collects are said or sung at Morning and Evening Prayer. However, in Advent and in Lent an additional collect should be said – the collect for the season. For example, on the second Sunday in Advent at Matins, the person officiating would say the collect for that Sunday and then follow it with the collect for the season. The other two set collects would then be said. The same applies to the 40 days of Lent, when the Ash Wednesday collect should be said at every service of Morning and Evening Prayer after the Collect for the Day and before the other two collects. This emphasizes the distinctive character of the season.

The State Prayers

The prayers that are laid out in the *Book of Common Prayer* to be said after the collects are commonly called the State Prayers. Written at various points in the history of the Prayer Book, they pray for the Monarch, the Royal Family, and the Clergy and People. They end with the Prayer of St Chrysostom and the Grace. It is a well-established custom now that the prayers for the Sovereign and the Royal Family are omitted when the service is used day-by-day (unless it is appropriate to say them because of some special connection with the Crown). The Uniformity Amendment Act of 1872 formally allowed the State Prayers to be omitted on certain occasions. Many people prefer to use a variety of other prayers instead to reflect the season or some other local concern. However, at times of national thanksgiving or need, the State Prayers are very powerful in expressing our common allegiance and unity as a nation.

If I want to add other prayers after the collects, can I?

Yes. It is very common to offer prayers for a whole range of different needs.

If I want prayers that are in keeping with the *Book of Common Prayer*, where can I find them?

A must-have for anyone who needs to lead prayers at a Prayer Book service is the first volume of *Parish Prayers*, edited by Frank Colquhoun. This contains hundreds of prayers written in Prayer Book language covering the range of the Christian year and all sorts of special needs and circumstances.

Conclusion

Both Morning and Evening Prayer end with the Grace from 2 Corinthians 13. This can be said by the person officiating or by the whole congregation. It is quite permissible to conclude the service with an alternative form of words, perhaps a blessing if a priest is present or another appropriate sentence of scripture.

What about a sermon?

Although the rubric doesn't mention a sermon, sermons have been preached on Sundays at Morning and Evening Prayer for generations. If there is to be a sermon, it could go after the prayers and before the Grace (or blessing). On a Sunday, you may even have hymns. In which case, a hymn could be sung after the prayers and before the sermon, and after the sermon and before the conclusion.

4

Lighten our darkness, we beseech thee, O Lord
Evening Prayer (Evensong)

The basic structure of the service

- Opening Penitential Sentence.
- Penitential Introduction (Bidding, General Confession, Absolution, Lord's Prayer).
- Opening dialogue and 'Glory be to the Father . . .'.
- *Venite* (Psalm 95).
- Psalm(s) for the day.
- Old Testament Lesson.
- *Magnificat* (Song of the Blessed Virgin Mary) or *Cantate Domino* (Psalm 98).
- New Testament Lesson.
- *Nunc Dimittis* (the Song of Simeon) or *Deus Misereatur* (Psalm 67).
- Apostles' Creed.
- The Suffrages (including the Lord's Prayer and dialogue between minister and congregation).
- Collect for the Day followed by the two Evensong Collects.
- Prayers.
- Grace.

The service in detail

Penitential Introduction

Most of the rules, customs and possibilities that relate to Morning Prayer also relate to Evening Prayer, so please see the guidance above.

Canticles

Because Evensong is an amalgamation of the monastic services of Vespers and Compline, it means that the canticles are different from those in Morning Prayer. The shape of the service, however, is almost identical. The Song of Mary is given its Latin name *Magnificat* and the *Nunc Dimittis* is the Song of Simeon. However, alternatives are provided in the form of Psalm 98 and Psalm 67 – both of which are rarely used in favour of the more familiar and popular 'Mag and Nunc'.

Said or Sung

The Prayer Book often makes reference to texts being said or sung. This means that a lot of the service of Matins and Evensong can be sung if you wish. Composers have for hundreds of years set the words of the *Book of Common Prayer* to music. In addition to singing the parts of the liturgy, congregational hymns can be sung at both Morning and Evening Prayer.

At Evening Prayer hymns can be sung:

- after the opening dialogue and before the Psalm for the day (this is often called the Office Hymn)
- after the Third Collect and before the Prayers
- after the prayers and before the sermon, and/or after the sermon and before the conclusion of the service.

5

Take This Holy Sacrament to Your Comfort
Holy Communion

You are likely to find yourself leading worship in a church where Holy Communion is celebrated regularly using the *Book of Common Prayer*. That may be an early morning service ('the 8 o'clock') or the principal Sunday service. Either way, it is likely that the Prayer Book will be an established and valued part of the worship in that place.

Knowing a little more about Holy Communion – how the service fits and hangs together, what should be included and what can be left out and so on – is an important part of feeling confident in praying the Prayer Book Communion.

In *Common Worship*, the structure of each service is helpfully laid out so that we can understand the larger framework of the liturgy and how each piece relates to the next to form a whole. The Prayer Book doesn't easily fall into the four-fold *Common Worship* pattern, because it was written in a much earlier age before the liturgical reforms of the twentieth century. However, the *Book of Common Prayer* Communion still has a distinctive shape. That shape is set out here using some of the headings found in *Common Worship*.

The structure of the service

Prayers of Preparation

- Lord's Prayer (short form).
- Collect for Purity.

Penitential Introduction

- Ten Commandments.

Liturgy of the Word

- Collect for the Sovereign.
- Collect for the Day.
- Epistle.
- Gospel.
- Creed.
- Sermon.

Offertory Sentence and Preparation of the Holy Table

- Offertory Sentences.

Prayers of Intercession

- Prayers 'for the Church Militant here in earth'.

Exhortations

Prayers of Penitence

- Invitation to Confession.
- General Confession.
- Absolution.

Eucharistic Prayer

- Comfortable Words.
- Prayer of Consecration:
  - *Sursum Corda* ('Lift up you hearts').
  - Proper Preface (*there are five of these short paragraphs to be used on designated Feasts and Festivals*).
  - Prayer of Humble Access.
  - Consecration.

Giving of Communion

- Words of Administration.

Post Communion Prayers

- Lord's Prayer (long version).
- Prayer of Thanksgiving (choice of two).

Conclusion

- Gloria.
- Blessing.

The service in detail

It is worth stressing that there is more flexibility in the use of the *Book of Common Prayer* Holy Communion than you might first think. It would be easy to get the impression that this and other Prayer Book services are fixed and inflexible, that they must be done 'by the book'. However, we should remember that ever since 1549 the *Book of Common Prayer* has been used and interpreted with flexibility. Here is some guidance to help you know what should be kept in and what can be left out of the Order for the Holy Communion.

Prayers of Preparation

Lord's Prayer and Collect for Purity

Both these prayers go to make up an act of preparation to be said by the priest alone before celebrating Communion. Strictly speaking, they are not part of the Communion, only a preparation for it. This was Cranmer's way of reflecting in his new Prayer Book what happened in the medieval service commonly used in England in the sixteenth century. The medieval services had a much fuller rite of priestly preparation that involved confessions and so on, which Cranmer simplified and incorporated into his service book.

These preparatory prayers are intended to be said by the priest alone. The rubric (guidance note in *italics* in the *Book of Common Prayer*) at the beginning of the service directs the priest to say it 'at the north side of the Table', with the people kneeling. This position at the north end of the altar is very rare today. Most clergy will say these prayers from 'in the midst' of the Holy Table itself or from wherever the first part of the service is usually conducted. This could be a stall, the chancel step, or some other place.

Do these prayers have to be said by the priest alone?

No. Although the rubrics say they should, there is flexibility here to begin the service with one or both of these prayers said congregationally. Your options are:

- following the rubric
- saying the Lord's Prayer congregationally with the Collect for Purity said by the priest alone
- Saying the Lord's Prayer alone and saying the Collect for Purity congregationally
- saying it all congregationally.

The Collect for Purity is a good prayer for people to be encouraged to learn by heart, especially candidates for confirmation.

Penitential Introduction

Ten Commandments

The next part of the service is penitential in character. In the Second Prayer Book of 1552, the Ten Commandments were inserted at this point into the Communion and they have remained part of the *Book of Common Prayer* ever since. Each Commandment is recited by the priest and is followed by a response made by the whole congregation. The response is the same for Commandments 1–9. The tenth Commandment has a slightly different congregational response.

Do the Ten Commandments have to be said each time Communion is celebrated?

No. It is rare for the Commandments to be recited at each celebration of Communion, though some people do use the Prayer Book in that way. Use your discretion in deciding whether or not to say them. One rule that can be helpful is that the Commandments are said in Advent and Lent only – penitential seasons. This can be effective as it brings variation into the service and alters the mood of the liturgy, making it more penitential. This works well. They're more fitting at solemn times, so think about using them then.

If I decide to leave out the Ten Commandments, what could I use instead?

The Summary of the Law. It's a long-established practice to substitute the Summary for the Commandments. The Summary is much shorter and it makes perfect sense for the Commandments to be summarized by Christ's own words. The congregational response to the Summary of the Law is the same as to the last of the Commandments: 'Lord, have mercy upon us, and write all these thy laws in our hearts, we beseech thee.'

There are even alternatives to the Summary. Some use the Beatitudes, others use the Comfortable Words, and many use the simple form of the *Kyrie eleison* in Greek or in English ('Lord, have mercy upon us'). Any of these works well.

The important thing to remember in choosing an alternative to the Commandments is that the Communion begins in the Prayer Book with a strong sense that we approach God in humility and through penitence. It might disrupt the service too much if the Commandments were omitted altogether and nothing put in their place.

The Liturgy of the Word

Cranmer would not have known the phrase 'Liturgy of the Word', which we use today to identify that section of a service where the scriptures are read and their meaning explored, but it is a helpful title to identify the section of the *Book of Common Prayer* Communion that begins with the collects and finishes with the sermon.

Collects (pronounced *collects* not *collects*)

The collects in the Prayer Book are one of its finest features. They are ancient prayers, many of them from the early centuries of the Church, and their translation out of Latin is largely down to Archbishop Cranmer, who also composed some additional collects to add to the new Prayer Book (for example the First Sunday in Advent). In addition to the Collect for the Day, Cranmer composed and introduced to the Communion two collects for the Monarch. One of these two prayers was intended to be said at each celebration.

Prayer for the Monarch

Almighty God, whose kingdom is ever-lasting, and power infinite: Have mercy upon the whole Church; and so rule the heart of thy chosen servant, *ELIZABETH*, our Queen and Governor, that she (knowing whose minister she is) may above all things seek thy honour and glory: and that we and all her subjects (duly considering whose authority she hath) may faithfully serve, honour, and humbly obey her, in thee, and for thee, according to thy blessed Word and ordinance; through Jesus Christ our Lord, who with thee and the Holy Ghost liveth and reigneth, ever one God, world without end. Amen.

> **Do I need to say both the Collect for the Queen and the Collect for the Day?**
>
> No. Many people say both, praying for the Sovereign and then saying the Collect for the Day straight afterwards, but you can decide to omit the first collect. You should never leave out the Collect for the Day. Of the two, the Collect for the Day is the essential part of the service. However, the Collect for the Monarch is very appropriate on certain days and at certain times, especially at times of national celebration or national need.
>
> Many clergy would introduce the Collect for the Day with 'The Lord be with you' or 'Let us pray'. Again, this is down to your discretion and custom.

Collect, Epistle and Gospel

The Prayer Book has within its covers all you need to conduct a service of the Holy Communion. This was Cranmer's ideal; he objected to the number and complexity of the books required to lead any service in his own time and so composed a book that stood alone. That is why he incorporated all the necessary readings for Communion into the *Book of Common Prayer*. This means that for every Sunday of the year and for many feast days throughout the year, a complete set of readings is provided with an accompanying collect.

These are arranged quite simply. The readings begin with the first Sunday of the Church's year (Advent Sunday) and work through the year to the last Sunday of the Church's year (Twenty-Fifth Sunday after Trinity). Following the Sunday readings come the readings for saints days and other feast days. These are similarly arranged. They begin in Adventtide (St Andrew's Day) and work through the year to All Saints' Day.

There is even guidance in the form of a rubric (guidance note in *italics*) about what you should do if there happens to be more than twenty-five Sundays after Trinity. The advice in that instance is to go back to the readings for Epiphany and use the Collects, Epistles and Gospel readings that weren't used first time around.

Once the collect has been prayed, the reading from the Epistle follows. It may come as a surprise to some that the readings for the Communion in the *Book of Common Prayer* don't include a reading from the Old Testament or a Psalm. This is not a mistake on Cranmer's part but only a reflection of the custom of an earlier time only to have an Epistle and Gospel reading at the Communion. The Old Testament, in the Prayer Book's scheme for reading the Bible, is read through once every year at Morning and Evening Prayer but not at Communion. There is only one example in the *Book of Common Prayer* (Ash Wednesday) when the Epistle for the day is actually a passage from the Old Testament – Joel.

The Prayer Book is designed to be easy to use by giving clear guidance about the essential things you need to know. It even gives guidance on how the Epistle at Communion is to be announced and concluded: 'The Epistle [or, portion of Scripture appointed for the Epistle] is written in the . . . Chapter of the . . . beginning at the – verse'. And after the Epistle the reader is to say 'Here endeth the Epistle.'

In the same way, guidance is given for the announcing of the Gospel: 'The holy Gospel is written in the . . . Chapter of the . . . beginning at the . . . verse.'

Some people are surprised that the *Book of Common Prayer* does not provide set congregational responses for the reading of the Gospel at the Communion, but that is not to say that a response isn't traditionally made. In many churches, the congregation responds to the announcement of the Gospel with 'Glory be to thee, O Lord' and at the conclusion of the Gospel with 'Praise be to thee, O Christ'. You should feel free to use those responses if you wish.

Do I have to follow the Prayer Book's readings for Communion?

This is a subject that divides opinion. Some clergy would prefer that the readings at a Prayer Book Communion are the same as those at the Principal Sunday Service. This means that everyone in the parish is following the same cycle of readings each Sunday (it also means that the clergy don't have to write two sermons!). The question you need to ask yourself is to what extent the readings at a Prayer Book service should be in the same 'register' or style of English as the rest of the service. Some feel strongly that the readings should be in the same style so that the integrity of the service is not disrupted by two quite different 'registers' of English. Sensitivity to the feelings of those worshipping at a Prayer Book service ought to be taken into account when making this decision. It is important to remember that for many people the Prayer Book readings form as much a part of their worship and spirituality as the words of the service itself.

Creed and Sermon

To those more familiar with the *Common Worship* order of Communion, the Nicene Creed and Sermon in the *Book of Common Prayer* will appear to be the wrong way around. In the *Book of Common Prayer* the Creed comes first and the sermon follows. A sermon doesn't always have to be preached, especially if the service is an early morning service – that is a matter of your choice and local custom – and the Creed can be omitted if it is a weekday. The Creed should not be omitted on a Sunday.

Be careful when saying the Creed as it appears in the Prayer Book! It sometimes catches people out. There are one or two of the words and phrases that are different in the version of the Nicene Creed used in the 1662 book. For example, the *Book of Common Prayer* version (which only uses the traditional 'I' form of the Creed) has, 'And I believe one Catholick and Apostolic Church' whereas most people would be familiar with 'And I believe in one holy catholic and apostolic Church.' If you are leading the Creed at Communion, make sure to read it through in advance.

If you are following the rubrics strictly, between the Creed and the Sermon the 'Curate' (the one who has been given the 'cure of souls' by the Bishop) should 'declare unto the people what Holy-days . . . are in the week following . . . and Briefs, Citations, and Excommunications read'. I would suggest you try not to make a habit of declaring excommunications at the Communion!

Offertory Sentence and Prayers

The *Book of Common Prayer* also follows a different order when it comes to the Offertory – that part of the service when a collection is taken and the altar is prepared with bread and wine ready for consecration.

In the *Book of Common Prayer*, the Offertory begins with the priest saying one or more of the Offertory Sentences. The Prayer Book's emphasis is always consciously scriptural, so as many as 20 suitable Bible passages are given at this point.

Do I have to use all the sentences?

No. You can choose one or perhaps two, but all 20 might be too much!

Once the Offertory Sentence has been read, the altar is pre-pared with 'so much Bread and Wine as [the priest] shall think sufficient'.

The priest then goes on to say: 'Let us pray for the whole state of Christ's Church militant here in earth.' This short introduction is the reason why the prayers of intercession in the *Book of Common Prayer* are known as the Prayers for the Church Militant. In the Prayer Book, the intercessions are fixed, and no seasonal variations exist.

Can I adapt the Prayers for the Church Militant?

Yes you can. In many places, the Prayers for the Church Militant are introduced by a bidding at the beginning. Before reading the prayers, the celebrant might invite (or 'bid') the congregation to pray for particular situations or people that are relevant to that place and time (such as 'As we bring our prayers before God, let us pray for the work and mission of this church, and for N and N who are sick at this time', and so on). The best biddings are short and serve not as alternative intercessions or a sermon but as simple suggestions for prayer that people can hold before God as the set prayers are read by the priest.

In addition, the prayers can be adapted by incorporating into the text the names of those who are sick or in need. This can be done sympathetically and discreetly: 'And we most humbly beseech thee of thy goodness, O Lord, to comfort and succour all them, who in this transitory life are in trouble, sorrow, need, sickness or any other adversity [remembering especially at this time N and N].'

In a similar way, the names of the departed can be remembered with thanksgiving – if that is the custom of your parish – in the following sentence: 'And we also bless thy holy name for all they servants departed this life in thy faith and fear [remembering N and N]; beseeching thee to give us grace so to follow their good examples.'

If you are used to freer intercessions, or intercessions broken up by congregational responses, then these prayers may seem stiff – they're written in continuous prose and are to be said by the priest alone without congregational participation. However, the advantage of this is that there is great comfort in knowing that these prayers have been used in this form for many generations. These are words that have carried the prayers of many Christians who have gone before us, and by using them today we are standing in a tradition of prayer that goes back centuries. That in itself strengthens and encourages us to pray.

Exhortations

The exhortations seem a little odd and out of place to us today. It is true that the exhortations (there are three in total) are very rarely used in public worship.

What are the Exhortations?

They are passages that were written with the intention of encouraging (or 'exhorting') the congregation to receive the sacrament 'worthily' and with proper devotion and preparation. Cranmer was very keen to encourage Christians to receive communion more regularly and more devoutly, with a clearer sense of what they were receiving and how 'esteemed' the sacrament of Communion is. In a sense, the exhortations serve as short sermons on why it is good to receive Communion and to do so after careful thought and self-examination.

First Exhortation

Each exhortation is slightly different. The first exhortation announces when the next celebration of Communion will be and exhorts the congregation to attend and to examine themselves beforehand in order that they receive communion devoutly and humbly: 'My duty is to exhort you in the mean season to consider the dignity of that holy mystery, and the great peril of the unworthy receiving thereof; and so to search and examine your own consciences, and that not lightly . . . but so that ye may come holy and clean to such a heavenly Feast.'

If a person feels they cannot receive communion because they do not have a 'quiet conscience', then they are encouraged to 'receive the benefit of absolution, together with ghostly [spiritual] counsel and advice'.

Second Exhortation

This one is written for a slightly different purpose and is intended to be used if the priest 'see the people negligent to come to the Holy Communion'. The tone of the exhortation is rather stern. The congregation is warned to 'take ye good heed, lest ye, withdrawing yourselves from the holy Supper, provoke God's indignation against you. It is an easy matter for a man to say, I will not communicate, because I am otherwise hindered by worldly business.' The congregation is left in no doubt that if they refuse to make their communion then they do 'great injury unto God'. This exhortation is an admonition – a ticking-off.

Third Exhortation

Of the three this is the most accessible and usable exhortation. It is more positive in tone, it doesn't refer to when the next celebration of Communion will be, as the others do, and is more general in its content. The congregation is still asked 'to try and examine themselves before they presume to eat of that Bread, and drink of that Cup', but the exhortation goes on to celebrate the benefits of communion in rich and memorable language: 'we dwell in Christ and he in us; we are one with Christ and he with us'. It also exhorts the congregation to consider that 'above all things' they must 'give most humble and hearty thanks to God' for the 'redemption of the world by the death and passion of our Saviour Christ, both God and man'.

This exhortation has not fallen entirely out of use. It is among the Prayer Book texts included in *Common Worship*.

Can I use it in a service?

It is very rare now for any of the exhortations to be used in a normal celebration of Holy Communion. However, because there is good teaching as well as rich and memorable imagery in the third exhortation, it can be a good idea for it to be printed as a text the congregation can read before the service begins, perhaps on the inside cover of an Order of Service (if a separate one is printed). Like many texts from the Prayer Book that are challenging for us to use in the liturgy itself, that doesn't mean that they cannot be used for instruction or preparation in a more imaginative way. That way they still retain their original purpose to help prepare Christians for Communion.

Prayers of Penitence

Prayers of Penitence is a heading familiar to all who use *Common Worship*; it is not a phrase that appears in the *Book of Common Prayer*. Nevertheless, it is a good way of describing what comes at this point in the Holy Communion. The service begins, as we have seen, with a Penitential Introduction (Ten Commandments or alternative), but unlike the structure of many services today (where the confession and absolution come near the beginning of the service), in the *Book of Common Prayer* the Prayers of Penitence come at the mid-point of the service immediately before the Eucharistic Prayer.

The Prayers of Penitence in the *Book of Common Prayer* consist of three parts:

- Invitation to Confession.
- General Confession.
- Absolution.

Invitation to Confession

The Invitation to Confession was originally written by Thomas Cranmer as an English supplement to the Latin Mass in order that those who were to receive communion according to the Latin service would at least understand the need to confess their sins and be ready to receive that sacrament. Cranmer wanted them to do this in English (evidence of just how much importance the Reformers placed upon approaching God through conscious penitence and humility). The invitation is said by the priest facing the people.

'Meekly kneeling upon your knees'. These are the words that bring the invitation to confession to an end. Kneeling is the classic Prayer Book posture, though it is less common today. The rubrics (guidance notes) in the *Book of Common Prayer* very often direct people to kneel. Kneeling is the Prayer Book's position for all prayer. It is also the posture that most vividly reminds us that before God we must be humble and contrite. In fact if you are following the rubrics strictly, then you will spend most of the Communion on your knees:

Kneel	Prayers of Preparation
	Commandments/Summary
	Collect(s)
Sit	Epistle
Stand	Gospel
	Creed
Sit	Sermon
Stand	Offertory
Kneel	Prayers for the Church Militant
	Invitation to Confession
	Confession
	Comfortable Words
	Eucharistic Prayer
	Communion
	Lord's Prayer
	Post Communion Prayer
	Gloria (often said kneeling if it is a said service)
	Blessing

Do I have to kneel as often as the *Book of Common Prayer* says?

No. Many find the traditional posture impractical and uncomfortable for a number of reasons. Kneeling for an extended period of time can be difficult, so please be pragmatic. For example, if your parish is used to standing to pray, then it would be best to keep with that tradition. It is important to remember that many of the directions in the Prayer Book relate to liturgical practice that may not easily translate to our own time. For many people kneeling is still the usual posture for prayer, but to those for whom it isn't, discretion can and should be exercised.

General Confession

The General Confession is called 'General' because it is said by everyone and is intended to be a corporate confession for everyone's sins. Cranmer and his fellow Reformers worked hard to encourage confession before receiving communion, and so brought confession into the service itself. The Reformers felt that it was wrong not to confess your sins sincerely before receiving Communion. To those familiar with the standard confession in *Common Worship*, the phrases in the General Confession in the *Book of Common Prayer* will be familiar, especially 'forgive us all that is past' and 'newness of life'.

Absolution

'Then shall the Priest (or the Bishop, being present) stand up, and turning himself to the people, pronounce this Absolution.' This is one of the texts that clergy should try to learn by heart, because it is to be said facing the people. If the altar is arranged so that the priest faces the people, this may not be so important, but for those facing east to celebrate Communion, it will be necessary to turn away from the book at this point. The words of the Absolution will be quite familiar because many of the phrases have been incorporated in the standard *Common Worship* absolution. The *Book of Common Prayer* gives no indication about the gesture a priest should adopt when saying the Absolution: some make the sign of the cross, others hold up a hand but do not make the sign of the cross, others make no gesture at all.

Comfortable Words

The Comfortable Words follow immediately after the Absolution, and form a bridge between the Prayers of Penitence and the Eucharistic Prayer. They are sentences from scripture to encourage and prepare the worshipper for communion by stating the grace and promise that Christ brings.

The Eucharistic Prayer

The term Eucharistic Prayer is another term that Cranmer would not have known or used, but it has become very familiar to us today. The Prayer of Consecration, as it is called in the *Book of Common Prayer*, was once part of a much longer prayer that more closely reflected the consecration from the medieval service.

The opening dialogue between priest and congregation is called the *Sursum Corda*, from the Latin 'Lift up your hearts'. Unlike the Eucharistic Prayers in *Common Worship*, the *Sursum Corda* in the Prayer Book is missing the opening greeting, 'The Lord be with you'. In many cases clergy insert this into the *Sursum Corda* because they feel that the opening dialogue is incomplete without it. This is certainly an option for you.

The beginning of the Prayer of Consecration (often called the Preface) then follows the Sursum Corda with the words, 'It is very meet, right, and our bounden duty . . .'. The *Book of Common Prayer* then provides five proper prefaces to be used at certain times of the year (Christmas Day and seven days after; Easter Day and seven days after; Ascension Day and seven days after; Whitsunday and six days after; Upon the Feast of Trinity only). These proper prefaces are there to be used on certain appropriate feast days in the year. The reason that all but one of the proper prefaces are used for the day itself and also for the seven days following reflects the ancient custom of keeping the octave of a feast (the day and a whole seven days after). These texts are called proper prefaces because they preface, or introduce, the actual Prayer of Consecration over the bread and wine – the central part of the Eucharistic Prayer.

The congregational response 'Holy, Holy, Holy, Lord God of Hosts' is called the *Sanctus* (from the Latin of the original). Even though it was removed in 1552, in many places an additional sentence is added to the *Sanctus* to make the *Benedictus* ('Blessed is he that cometh in the name of the Lord. Hosanna in the highest'). The choice whether or not to use the *Benedictus* is still for some a matter of eucharistic theology and churchmanship. However, the *Benedictus* remains an option for those who wish to add it to the Eucharistic Prayer.

The earlier chapters of this book set out the reasons why the Eucharistic Prayer in the *Book of Common Prayer* is as it is. During 1549–52, this section of the service changed dramatically. After 1552, the long action of the consecration was broken up into several parts in order to make it clear that this service was not the medieval Mass.

For that reason, once the Eucharistic Prayer has been started, it suddenly stops again, and the priest then says a prayer on behalf of the whole congregation: 'Then shall the Priest, kneeling down at the Lord's Table, say in the name of all them that shall receive Communion this Prayer following.' The Prayer of Humble Access, as it has become known, is a core text to Anglicans, and it features in Anglican Prayer Books all around the world.

> ### Does the Prayer of Humble Access have to be said 'in the name of all'?
>
> No. Although the rubric states that it should be said by the priest alone, the prayer can be said congregationally if you wish. In many places that is what happens. When it is said congregationally it creates a sense of preparation and expectation that adds something to the liturgy. If it is to be said in this way it should be said softly and with sensitivity, not declaimed loudly.

Prayer of Humble Access

We do not presume to come to this thy Table, O merciful Lord, trusting in our own righteousness, but in thy manifold and great mercies. We are not worthy so much as to gather up the crumbs under thy Table. But thou art the same Lord, whose property is always to have mercy: Grant us therefore, gracious Lord, so to eat the flesh of thy dear Son Jesus Christ, and to drink his blood, that our sinful bodies may be made clean by his body, and our souls washed through his most precious blood, and that we may evermore dwell in him, and he in us. Amen.

The Prayer of Consecration

This prayer is short and simple, and since 1662 it has been provided with a variety of useful rubrics to direct the priest to do certain things at certain points. These rubrics refer to the manual acts – what the hands of the priest should do during the consecration. They are written into the *Book of Common Prayer* to ensure that as the narrative of the Last Supper is recited by the priest, the appropriate elements are taken into the priest's hands.

To some, the Prayer of Consecration seems startlingly short, especially compared with the other Eucharistic Prayers that are used in the Church of England today. That is because it is the first part of a longer prayer that has been divided up over time. The second part of this prayer is now a Post Communion Prayer found later in the service.

Communion

After the Amen of the Prayer of Consecration, the *Book of Common Prayer* provides no texts or guidance other than that the Minister should receive communion first and then distribute to other clergy and then to the congregation after them.

Can I say something at this point?

Yes. In certain places the *Agnus Dei* is said (or sung) immediately after the consecration. If it is to be said then the *Agnus Dei* can be said by the priest alone as the consecrated elements are prepared for distribution, or said congregationally, or said as a dialogue between priest and people. It is called the *Agnus Dei* because those are the opening Latin words of the eucharistic hymn 'O Lamb of God, that takest away the sins of the world, have mercy upon us/grant us thy peace'.

If parts of the service are sung, then the *Agnus Dei* could be sung by a cantor or a choir, or even sung congregationally.

In the *Book of Common Prayer,* there is also no invitation to communion or any formal words immediately before the giving of communion. The Prayer Book simply provides words to be said at the distribution of communion.

Can I invite people to communion?

Yes. If you want to do that then these words are often used: 'Draw near with faith. Receive the body of our Lord Jesus

---

Christ which he gave for you, and his blood which he shed for you. Eat and drink in remembrance that he died for you, and feed on him in thy heart by faith with thanksgiving.' These words are provided in *Common Worship* and are commonly used at Prayer Book services. Although none are provided in the *Book of Common Prayer*, words of invitation can be helpful in giving worshippers confidence to come forward.

Words of Distribution

Where the *Book of Common Prayer* lacks in words of invitation to Communion, it more than makes up in the words to be said at the distribution of Communion! Strictly speaking, the full words of distribution should be said each time to each communicant, but for obvious reasons it is rarely possible or practical to do this. Today there is flexibility in what you can say when distributing Holy Communion.

What should I say when giving Communion?

It is helpful to learn the words of distribution so that you can say them with confidence. For many who have worshipped for years according to the Prayer Book, it is part of their worship and devotion to hear the *Book of Common Prayer* words of distribution instead of the more usual 'The Body/Blood of Christ'. A good rule to follow is the one set out in *Common Worship* Order Two: 'When occasion requires, these words may be said once to each row of communicants, or to a convenient number within each row.'

If you wish to use both sentences when administering the consecrated elements, then it can be helpful to say the first sentence to the first communicant and the second sentence to the next (still in the hearing of the first), alternating along the row. This means that most people in a row will hear these familiar and powerful words spoken.

The great strength of the *Book of Common Prayer* is that it's liturgical formulas carefully express the balanced mind of the church, and so are able to hold together in communion people whose eucharistic theology is inspired by different traditions.

Lord's Prayer

Most people are familiar with the Lord's Prayer coming immediately after the Amen of the Eucharistic Prayer. The Prayer Book has it in a different place. In the *Book of Common Prayer* the Lord's Prayer comes after not before receiving communion, and it is to be said only once all have received the sacrament. In the Prayer Book, the Lord's Prayer is almost like a Post Communion Prayer. At this point it is said in its long form.

The Post Communion Prayers

Following the Lord's Prayer come two very fine prayers. You have a choice which one to use. The first prayer is known as the Prayer of Oblation. The Prayer of Oblation once formed the second part of the prayer of consecration. It is a prayer that offers to God (the meaning of oblation) 'this our sacrifice of praise and thanksgiving'. Thankfully, the Prayer of Oblation was not done away with, but simply moved to its position after communion.

The second prayer is generally called the Prayer of Thanksgiving because it begins: 'Almighty and everliving God, we most heartily thank thee, for thou dost vouchsafe to feed us . . . with the spiritual food of the most precious body and blood of thy Son . . .' Both prayers are very rich in theological and spiritual meaning.

The Gloria

Another puzzling thing for those coming to the *Book of Common Prayer* for the first time is the position of the *Gloria in excelsis.* In modern liturgies the *Gloria* comes near the beginning of the Communion, before the Collect for the Day. In the *Book of Common Prayer* the *Gloria* was given a place at the very end of the service and serves as a concluding hymn of praise to God. The direction given in the Prayer Book is that the *Gloria* can be 'said or sung'.

The General Blessing

The Peace in the Prayer Book is found right at the end of Communion and forms part of the General Blessing: 'The peace of God which passeth all understanding keep your hearts and minds in the knowledge and love of God, and of his Son Jesus Christ our Lord . . .' These words have been a distinctive feature of Anglican liturgies ever since.

Priest and Minister

The advice in this book refers frequently to what the priest does. The use of 'priest' isn't intended to make a particular point about ordained ministry. It is the language the Prayer Book uses in most places throughout Holy Communion. In a few places, 'minister' is referred to, but the Prayer Book, despite attempts to revise it in a more Protestant direction, still retains frequent references to priest in relation to the sacraments.

What if there isn't a priest?

It is frequently the case that worship will not always be led by a priest because one isn't available. Many others exercise a ministry to lead worship under the authority of the bishop. If it is the pattern of a church to have the *Book of Common Prayer* Holy Communion on a certain Sunday in the month and a priest cannot be present, what are the options?

Ante-Communion

Ante-Communion is the traditional name given to the form of service that Communion takes when a priest is not present to celebrate. Ante-Communion simply means 'before Communion', and refers to that part of the Communion service that can properly be taken by a lay person. It is an option that the Prayer Book gives guidance on.

There are certain key things in the Communion that only a priest can do:

- Absolve people from their sins.
- Say the Eucharistic Prayer.
- Pronounce the General Blessing.

If a priest is not available, then you would need to omit those parts of the service that only a priest is authorized to do. Without a priest to celebrate, the service should follow this pattern:

- Prayers of Preparation.
- Prayers of Penitence.
- Collect(s).
- Readings.
- Creed.
- Sermon.
- Offertory (during which only a collection should be taken).
- Prayers 'for the Church Militant'.
- Final Collect(s) provided for Ante-Communion. These are at the very back of the service of Holy Communion.

The *Book of Common Prayer* supplies up to six different collects that can be used to conclude a service of Ante-Communion. These collects are intended to provide an appropriate conclusion to Communion in the absence of a priest.

Two prayers that can be said at the end of Ante-Communion

Grant, we beseech thee, Almighty God, that the words, which we have heard this day with our outward ears, may through thy grace be so grafted inwardly in our hearts, that they may bring forth in us the fruit of good living, to the honour and praise of thy Name; through Jesus Christ our Lord. Amen.

Almighty God, who hast promised to hear the petitions of them that ask in thy Son's Name: We beseech thee mercifully to incline thine ears to us that have made now our prayers and supplications unto thee; and grant that those things, which we have faithfully asked according to thy will, may effectually be obtained, to the relief of our necessity, and to the setting forth of thy glory; through Jesus Christ our Lord. Amen.

Music and Holy Communion

If Prayer Book Communion is to be the principal Sunday service (that is, not a said early morning service), then it would be a good thing to have music in order to enrich the worship. The *Book of Common Prayer* Holy Communion has been sung for many generations, which means that a great deal of music exists for this and other Prayer Book services. The Royal School of Church Music (RSCM) would be a very helpful organization to contact for advice and further information on how best to choose music for a Prayer Book service.

Hymns

Hymns can easily be fitted into the framework of the Holy Communion, just like any other service. Here are some suggestions where the hymns might go:

- Hymn.
- Prayers of Preparation.

- Penitential Introduction.
- Collect(s).
- Epistle.
- Hymn (often called the Gradual Hymn).
- Gospel.
- Creed.
- Sermon.
- Offertory Hymn (this could be sung as the collection is taken and the altar prepared).
- Prayers 'for the Church Militant'.
- Prayers of Penitence.
- Eucharistic Prayer.
- Communion (hymns can be sung during the distribution).
- Lord's Prayer.
- Post Communion Prayer.
- Gloria (this could be sung).
- General Blessing.
- Final Hymn.

If you also wish to sing the set texts of the Communion service (such as the *Sursum Corda, Sanctus,* Lord's Prayer, *Gloria*), then these have over the years been set to music by a variety of composers in simple musical settings that most parish choirs could sing. The RSCM would be a helpful guide in this.

Merbecke's setting of the Communion texts

The year after the Prayer Book was first published, a setting in plainsong of the set texts of the Communion was compiled by John Merbecke. John Merbecke's setting from 1550 – simply known as 'Merbecke' to most people – has remained popular ever since and is still sung in many churches today. Merbecke can be found at the back of the *New English Hymnal* on p. 1221, where the plainsong melody has been provided with an organ accompaniment. In all but the most recent editions of the *New English Hymnal* the music for the set parts of the Communion is actually called 'Rite B' from the days when those Prayer Book texts formed part of Rite B in the *Alternative Service Book* (ASB).

The *Book of Common Prayer* Holy Communion as it appears in *Common Worship*

When *Common Worship* was being compiled, the Liturgical Commission made a deliberate decision to include a number of texts/services from the *Book of Common Prayer*. Morning and Evening Prayer as well as Holy Communion were among them. In *Common Worship Main Volume* (black cover), you can find the Prayer Book Daily Offices along with what is called Holy Communion Order Two.

Order Two is the service of Holy Communion that appears in two forms – contemporary and traditional language. The version in traditional language is the version of the *Book of Common Prayer* that the Liturgical Commission felt most accurately reflected how the *Book of Common Prayer* is actually used in churches up and down the land. Many of the tips and suggestions in this simple guide agree with the guidance given in Order Two. If you are coming to the Prayer Book for the first time, using Order Two is a good way of introducing yourself to the *Book of Common Prayer* Holy Communion. Order Two is laid out in a clear and accessible way. It is easy to follow on the page, and it honestly reflects what happens in most parishes when the *Book of Common Prayer* is used. Order Two lays out your options and choices very clearly – it is worth looking at, especially if you are in a parish where the only altar copy of the Prayer Book is in a poor state of repair.

1662/1928 Altar Books

In many parishes, the 1662 *Book of Common Prayer* Communion has been said from a large–print priest's copy that has also contained the alternative services 'proposed in 1928'. Many of these books were printed. This may be confusing for anyone who is unfamiliar with the *Book of Common Prayer* 'proposed in 1928'.

In the years leading up to 1928, there was an attempt to revise the 1662 *Book of Common Prayer*. Many in the Church felt that the 1662 Prayer Book no longer met all the needs of a modern age. Therefore a number of alternative services were drafted (such as an alternative Morning and Evening Prayer, Holy Communion, Baptism, Marriage and Burial). These alternatives were intended to sit alongside the services of 1662 as an option for those who wished to use them. They were not intended to supplant the 1662 services.

The attempt to revise the *Book of Common Prayer* along these lines failed when the necessary legislation was voted down in the House of Commons, but by this stage many books had been published with the proposed 1928 materials alongside the 1662 services. These proposed alternatives were later authorized by individual bishops for use in their dioceses, which meant that the '1928 Prayer Book' became widely available and widely used, even though it was not the official Prayer Book of the Church. Don't be surprised if you find yourself leading a Prayer Book service from a book that contains services 'proposed in 1928'.

6

Steadfast in faith, joyful through hope, rooted in charity
Baptism

The 1662 *Book of Common Prayer* contains no fewer than three Baptism services:

- The Ministration of Publick Baptism of Infants to be used in the Church.
- The Ministration of Private Baptism of Children in Houses.
- The Ministration of Baptism to such as are of riper years and able to answer for themselves.

The reason there are three is purely practical:

- The service 'to be used in Church' is intended to be the standard service.
- The service authorized for use 'in Houses' simply reflects the fact that children at one time were born at home, and this was a form of service to be used – often by midwives – for those babies whose lives were to be short.
- The third service was written especially for the 1662 *Book of Common Prayer* with a view to those in England who, during Cromwell's Commonwealth (1649–60), had not been baptized because of the prevailing theology of the time, which had rejected the practice of infant baptism. It was also written for those abroad in the growing

colonies of North America who had been converted to Christianity in adulthood.

There has been so much liturgical scholarship about Baptism in the twentieth century that the *Book of Common Prayer* Baptism service has very largely fallen out of use because it does not reflect those scholarly insights. Not only have more recent rites revived symbolism in the Baptism service (oil, light as well as water), but Baptism in a number of churches is now regularly celebrated within the context of the Eucharist.

The Prayer Book Baptism service doesn't easily conform to these recent liturgical insights and practices. For example, the *Book of Common Prayer* Baptism service is intended to be a stand-alone service or to take place after the third collect at Morning or Evening Prayer, not within the Eucharist.

It was also composed for simplicity and to be free of many ceremonies and symbols. Yet its unfamiliarity might be its strength, and so too might its simplicity. The *Book of Common Prayer* Baptism is worth at least a second look.

The structure of the service

- Preface (Introduction).
- Collect.
- Collect.
- Short reading from St Mark.
- Exhortation based on the Gospel reading.
- Collect.
- Priest's address to Godparents.
- Godparents' promises and Apostles' Creed.
- Four short intercessions.
- Prayer over the Water.
- Baptism.
- Signing with the Cross.
- Prayer of Thanksgiving.
- Exhortation to Godparents.

You can see from this outline that the Baptism service is short, simple and to the point. It contains none of the symbolism of more recent Baptism services. In fact it came about precisely because Thomas Cranmer and others wanted to get back to something more 'primitive' (authentic) and felt that the proliferations of ceremonies and symbols surrounding the sacrament of Baptism had succeeded in obscuring its meaning. For that reason, the *Book of Common Prayer* Baptism service was stripped of those now recently revived ceremonies in favour of a straight-speaking theology of fallen human nature and salvation through grace alone. That theology of fall and redemption is presented within a simple structure and is accompanied by the clear exhortation for every baptized person to live a serious and devout Christian life.

How this service could be used in the parish today

- As it appears printed in the Prayer Book makes it very difficult for most people to find and follow – print a separate booklet.
- The whole text of the Baptism service can be found on the *Book of Common Prayer* section of the Church of England's liturgy pages. You can prepare your service from there.
- Don't feel that every word has to be said. This is often the mistake of those who use the Prayer Book. Take some time to read and become familiar with the service in advance. Know which parts of the service are essential and which not.

There are certain parts of the service that can legitimately be left out. This structure indicates what they might be:

- Preface (Introduction).
- *Collects – say one or the other, not both.*
- Short reading from St Mark.

- Exhortation based on the Gospel reading – *instead of this exhortation, a short address could be given on the same theme.*
- Collect – *this prayer asks for something already prayed for, so it could be omitted.*
- Priest's address to Godparents.
- Godparents' promises and Apostles' Creed.
- Four short intercessions – *say one or two of these, not four.*
- Prayer over the Water.
- Baptism.
- Signing with the Cross.
- Prayer of Thanksgiving.
- Exhortation to Godparents – *this could be printed in the Order of Service, or given to the Godparents in advance for them to read. It could form the basis of a discussion with the Godparents about their responsibilities and come as part of the baptism preparation.*

Because the service doesn't have a liturgical ending, a blessing could be pronounced after the prayer of thanksgiving, or another suitable prayer or dismissal could be said (such as the Grace).

Hymns

If there is an opportunity for hymns, then the service could incorporate them:

- at the beginning, after the opening introduction
- before the Prayer over the Water
- following the Prayer of Thanksgiving and before the Blessing.

7

To have and to hold from this day forward
Holy Matrimony

The words of the Prayer Book Marriage service (formally called 'The Form of Solemnization of Matrimony') are perhaps the most well-known and memorable in all the *Book of Common Prayer*. They have imprinted themselves on generations of English men and women.

The basic structure of the service

- Preface (Introduction).
- Declarations.
- Vows.
- Giving of the ring.
- Collect.
- Proclamation.
- Blessing.
- Psalm.
- Prayers.
- Collect.
- Sermon (optional).
- Declaration of Duties.

The service in detail

The structure of the 1662 Marriage service is very simple: it begins with an introduction that summarizes the Church's fundamental teaching on marriage, explains why 'matrimony was ordained', and gives an opportunity for legal objections to be raised.

After that introduction (called the Preface), the couple are asked to declare whether they are happy to continue to the vows, in the light of what they have heard. The vows are then made and a ring is given (the 1662 *Book of Common Prayer* works on the understanding that only one ring is to be given). Once the ring is given, then a collect is said and the couple's right hands are joined together (and often symbolically tied together by a stole) as the priest says, 'Those whom God hath joined together, let no man put asunder'. Once the 'tying of the knot' has been done, the minister pronounces that 'they be man and wife together', and then says a blessing over the couple.

The *Book of Common Prayer* then provides two Psalms to be said or sung as the couple go up to the 'Lord's Table' for the prayers. The prayers are in the form of a series of dialogues (versicles and responses), the Lord's Prayer in its short form (omitting 'For thine be the kingdom, the power and the glory. . .'), and four set prayers (the prayer for the gift of children can, as the rubric suggests, be 'omitted where the Woman is past child-bearing').

The 1662 Marriage service also provides some additional words that are to be used 'if there be no sermon'. These words serve as a short sermon on what the Prayer Book calls 'the duties of man and wife'. The service ends with the suggestion that 'the newly married persons should receive the Holy Communion at the time of their marriage, or at the first opportunity after their marriage'.

Is this the only version of the Prayer Book Marriage service?

No. There is another version that is commonly used as an alternative to the 1662 service. It is the version that first

---

appeared in the proposed Prayer Book of 1928, and that later became known as *Alternative Services, Series One: The Form of Solemnization of Matrimony.*

In what ways is this service different?

When the liturgists who worked on the proposed revision of the Prayer Book looked at the 1662 Marriage service, they saw that it contained a number of phrases that needed rewriting or refining, partly because the Church's understanding of marriage had changed in the preceding centuries, and partly because society's attitudes and expectations had changed. In addition, the structure of the 1662 service was felt to need some revising. For example, the 1662 Marriage service doesn't have a clear liturgical ending, so one was provided in the alternative service of 1928.

Where can I find *Alternative Services, Series One: The Form of Solemnization of Matrimony*?

Online:

- Visit the Church of England's homepage and click Prayer & Worship.
- Then click on Worship and you will be able to access all of the Church of England's liturgical texts.
- This gives you access to all the texts of the 1662 *Book of Common Prayer*, as well as *Common Worship.* Included under *Common Worship* are the Series One services for marriage and burial.

In print:

Series One services can be found in the second edition of *Common Worship: Pastoral Services* (green book). Series One services are also available from Church House Publishing in separate printed booklets. Marriage is in a yellow booklet, and burial in a purple booklet.

Why is it called Series One?

In July 1929, the Archbishop of Canterbury proposed that the services that had been put together for the proposed Prayer Book of 1928 should be used in the Church of England – even though the new liturgies had failed to get Parliamentary approval – because they were consistent with 'loyalty to the principles of the Church of England'. However, it wasn't until 1966 that these services from the 1928 *Book of Common Prayer* were legally authorized for use in public worship – some of them in an amended form. That is why they were called the First Series of Alternative Services.

Series Two and Series Three eventually led the way to the production of the *Alternative Service Book* in 1980.

Series One: Marriage

Basic structure of the service

- Introduction.
- The Marriage.
- The Blessing of the Marriage.

The service in detail

Introduction (Preface)

This welcomes people and explains why the congregation is 'gathered here in the sight of God'. It then sets out the Church's understanding of marriage and its importance (it is almost a mini sermon on marriage).

Once it has done this, the congregation is asked to make known any legal impediment to the marriage. The couple is then asked to make known 'any impediment, why ye may not be lawfully joined together in matrimony'.

In this opening section of the service, a number of words and phrases have been changed from the 1662 Prayer Book to make the Preface a little 'softer' and more understandable. The Series One Marriage service retains the style of language found in the 1662 *Book of Common Prayer* while sensitively revising some of the phrases to make them more relevant. A good example of this is the second of three reasons given for marriage:

- 1662 – 'for a remedy against sin and to avoid fornication; that such persons as have not the gift of continency might marry, and keep themselves undefiled members of Christ's body'.
- *Series One* – 'in order that the natural instincts and affections, implanted by God, should be hallowed and directed aright; that those who are called of God to this holy estate, should continue therein in pureness of living'.

The Marriage

This section begins with the declarations made by the couple. The declarations (the answers to which are 'I will' and not 'I do') express their desire to continue to the vows. The vows follow immediately after. This section of the service ends with the proclamation of the marriage and the nuptial blessing.

Declarations in the 1662 Book of Common Prayer

Here is an example of how the wording in Series One has been changed to make it more suited to the modern age. In the 1662 Prayer Book, the declarations ask one question to the groom and a slightly different one to the bride:

Bridegroom (1662):
N. wilt thou have this woman to thy wedded wife, to live together after God's ordinance in the holy estate of Matrimony? *Wilt thou love her, comfort her, honour, and keep her,* in sickness and in health; and, forsaking all other, keep thee only unto her, so long as ye both shall live?

Bride (1662):

> N. wilt thou have this man to thy wedded husband, to live together after God's ordinance in the holy estate of Matrimony? *Wilt thou obey him, and serve him, love, honour, and keep him,* in sickness and in health; and, forsaking all other, keep thee only unto him, so long as ye both shall live?

In the 1662 Prayer Book, the bride has to promise to 'obey', 'serve', 'love' and 'keep', whereas the groom promises to 'love', 'comfort', 'honour' and 'keep'. By comparison, in Series One the bride makes identical declarations to the groom. This makes their declarations equal and removes the expectations on the bride to 'obey'.

Declarations in Series One

Bride and Groom:

> N. wilt thou have this woman[man] to thy wedded wife[husband], to live together after God's law in the holy estate of Matrimony? *Wilt thou love her[him], comfort her[him], honour, and keep her[him],* in sickness and in health; and, forsaking all other, keep thee only unto her[him], so long as ye both shall live?

The declarations in Series One are also different from 1662 in another respect. The older word 'ordinance' is replaced with 'law'. This makes the language a little clearer.

'Giving away'

In *Common Worship*, the 'giving away' of the bride by her father or friend is removed in favour of an open invitation to both man and woman to make their vows. The *Book of Common Prayer* and Series One follow an older custom by asking, 'Who giveth this woman to be married to this man?' The answer to this question is the gesture of handing over the bride's right hand to the priest by her father or friend. The priest then passes it directly into the right hand of the groom for the vows to be said.

The vows in 1662

In the 1662 Marriage service, the vows are different for the bride and the groom.

> *Groom (1662):*
> I N. take thee N. to my wedded wife, to have and to hold from this day forward, for better for worse, for richer for poorer, in sickness and in health, to love and to cherish, till death us do part, according to God's holy ordinance; and thereto I plight thee my troth.

> *Bride (1662):*
> I N. take thee N. to my wedded husband, to have and to hold from this day forward, for better for worse, for richer for poorer, in sickness and in health, to love, cherish, and to obey, till death us do part, according to God's holy ordinance; and thereto I give thee my troth.

The presence of 'obey' in the 1662 vows echoes the declarations made beforehand in the 1662 version in which the bride also promises to obey. In Series One, the vows of bride and groom are also identical, like the declarations, and 'obey' has been removed. So too has 'ordinance' in favour of 'law'.

> *Groom (Series One):*
> I N. take thee N. to my wedded wife, to have and to hold from this day forward, for better for worse, for richer, for poorer, in sickness and in health, to love and to cherish, till death us do part, according to God's holy law; and thereto I give thee my troth.

Bride (Series One):
> I N. take thee N. to my wedded husband, to have and to hold from this day forward, for better for worse, for richer, for poorer, in sickness and in health, to love and to cherish, till death us do part, according to God's holy law; and thereto I give thee my troth.

What if a bride wants to say 'obey'?

Although Series One provides alternative vows to those of 1662, it also contains the provision for both the declarations and the vows from 1662 to be used if desired.

What does 'plight thee my troth' and 'give thee my troth' mean?

In both the 1662 Prayer Book and in Series One, the word 'troth' is used. In 1662, the groom 'plights' his 'troth' and the bride 'gives' her 'troth'. In Series One, both bride and groom 'give' their 'troth'. 'Troth' is an antique word for 'truth'. It also means 'promise'. The word 'plight' is an old word for 'pledge'. So when a couple give their troth to one another (as in Series One), they are giving their 'truth', their binding and solemn promise.

Wedding Ring

Both the 1662 service and Series One only provide for the exchange of a single wedding ring. However, this does not prevent two rings from being exchanged in the way that is common today.

One of the disadvantages of the Marriage service in the *Book of Common Prayer* is that it does not provide words for blessing the wedding ring. Series One, on the other hand, does provide a blessing for the priest to say over the ring before it is given:

> Bless, O Lord, this ring, and grant that he who gives it and she who shall wear it may remain faithful to each other, and

abide in thy peace and favour, and live together in love until their lives' end; through Jesus Christ our Lord. Amen.

Because this blessing is only intended to be said for one ring, it is written in the singular. It is easily amended if there is an exchange of rings.

Bless, O Lord, these rings, and grant that those who give and wear them may remain faithful to each other, and abide in thy peace and favour, and live together in love until their lives' end; through Jesus Christ our Lord. Amen.

This blessing can be further amended to incorporate the name of the couple, if you feel that would be a helpful thing to do.

Bless, O Lord, these rings, and grant that N *and N who give and wear them* may remain faithful to each other, and abide in thy peace and favour, and live together in love until their lives' end; through Jesus Christ our Lord. Amen.

Giving the wedding ring

Series One also changes a word or two in the giving of the ring to reflect a different (and more equal) attitude towards marriage.

1662:
With this ring I thee wed, with my body I thee worship, and with all my worldly goods I thee endow: In the Name of the Father, and of the Son, and of the Holy Ghost. Amen.

Series One:
With this ring I thee wed, with my body I thee *honour, and all my worldly goods with thee I share*: In the Name of the Father, and of the Son, and of the Holy Ghost. Amen.

There is greater balance in this. The intention to 'worship' with the body sounds an odd idea to more contemporary ears, so it is replaced with 'honour'. This is closer to the intended meaning of 'worship'. Also 'worldly goods' are not given by the man to the woman, but are shared between man and woman. This makes even more sense when these words are said when both man and woman are exchanging rings.

Collect, Proclamation and Nuptial Blessing
Collect

The collect that follows the giving of the rings is to be said while the couple are kneeling. It is almost identical in 1662 and Series One (Series One omits the biblical reference to Isaac and Rebecca, who 'lived faithfully together').

Although neither version of the collect makes reference to the couple by name, again it is possible to mention the couple by name, just as it is at the blessing of the rings. There are two appropriate places where this can be done (one or the other could be used, perhaps not both): 'Send thy blessing upon these thy servants, N and N, whom we bless in thy name' or 'that living faithfully together N and N may surely perform and keep the vow and covenant betwixt them made'. These are very minor changes to the collect but they can bring a personal touch to this formal service.

Because both 1662 and Series One are written with only one wedding ring in mind, when you use this service you need to remember to amend this collect slightly in order to refer to an exchange of rings. The words: 'whereof this ring given and received is a token and pledge' can easily be amended to 'whereof these rings given and received are tokens and pledges'.

Proclamation

Following the collect is the proclamation of the marriage – the point of the service that is for many the most dramatic – when for the first time they are declared 'man and wife'. This section also has to be amended very slightly if there is an exchange of rings as only the word 'ring' is printed in the text. Once the couple are proclaimed to be 'man and wife together', Cranmer inserted the sentence, 'Those whom God hath joined together, let no man put asunder.' This can be a dramatic gesture of unity, especially if the priest binds the right hands of the couple together with a stole, and lifts the hands sufficiently high for the whole congregation to see.

Blessing

The blessing (also called a benediction) that follows, which is identical in both 1662 and Series One, then seals the marriage with God's blessing.

The Blessing of the Marriage

Rather confusingly, the 'Blessing of the Marriage' is the name given to the section of the Marriage service in Series One that immediately follows the actual blessing (the nuptial blessing). It refers to the way the service goes on to bless the couple with prayers for them.

Psalms

First come the Psalms. The 1662 *Book of Common Prayer* provides two Psalms to be said or sung at this point (128 and 67). Series One provides an additional Psalm (37.3–7). The rubric says that these Psalms are 'suitable' not compulsory, which means that other Psalms could also be suitable.

Does a Psalm have to be said or sung at this point?

No. The *Book of Common Prayer* provides for a Psalm/Psalms to be said or sung, but that does not mean they are compulsory. A hymn, anthem or other piece of music would be just as appropriate at this point in the service.

The Psalm(s) allow for the priest and the couple to move to the altar for the prayers. In places where the altar has been brought forward into the nave, this movement may not be needed or may not be possible.

Prayers

The prayers themselves are simple and straightforward. They are broken into several sections:

- *Kyries* (Lord, have mercy upon us).
- Short form of the Lord's Prayer (omitting 'For thine is the kingdom, the power and the glory. . .').
- Series of versicles and responses (dialogues between priest and people).
- Prayers (there are five prayers in 1662, only four in Series One).

Once the final prayer has been said – it almost serves as an additional blessing – the service moves to its conclusion.

Conclusion

The 1662 Marriage service ends with a sermon. If there is no sermon, then the *Book of Common Prayer* provides for a declaration of duties to be read out. Unsurprisingly, this is rarely read out. The *Book of Common Prayer* also says that, if convenient, the Holy Communion should be celebrated. This might happen if the couple are regular communicants.

In Series One, there is clearer guidance about what to do to conclude the service:

- 'If there is Communion then the final prayer of those mentioned above is to be said just before the General Blessing at the Eucharist.'
- 'If there is no Communion . . . the Priest shall dismiss those that are gathered together.'

For this dismissal, a collect and a blessing is provided. These bring the service to a clear conclusion.

Marriage with Holy Communion (sometimes called a 'Nuptial Mass')

If I am using the 1662 service or Series One for the Marriage, what do I do if there is also a celebration of Prayer Book Holy Communion?

The *Book of Common Prayer* is unlike *Common Worship* in a variety of ways. The services in the *Book of Common Prayer* do not, for example, share the common structure that all services in *Common Worship* share. If a couple are being married according to the *Common Worship* Marriage service and wish for the Eucharist to be celebrated, then there is an easy way of conducting the marriage within the structure of the Eucharist. This is set out clearly in *Common Worship: Pastoral Services* (green book).

For the Prayer Book to be used in this way, the two services of Marriage and Holy Communion need to be fused together. Choosing precisely where and how to fuse them together leaves the priest with a degree of discretion.

One way of doing that is to conduct the marriage according to 1662/Series One from the beginning up to the nuptial blessing and then, perhaps after the singing of a hymn, to go into the Communion by saying the Collect for Marriage provided in Series One, and following it with the readings and the rest of the eucharistic liturgy. The prayers from the Marriage service can be inserted in the place of the Prayers for the Church Militant.

The structure of a Nuptial Mass according to the Prayer Book might look something like this:

1662 / Series One Marriage service

- Preface.
- Declarations.
- Vows.
- Giving of Rings.
- Nuptial Blessing.

Holy Communion

- Collect for Marriage.
- Epistle.
- Gospel.
- Creed (could be omitted at a wedding).
- Sermon.
- Offertory Sentence (during which the altar is prepared).
- Prayers from the Marriage service.
- Prayers of Penitence.
- Comfortable Sentences.
- Eucharistic Prayer.
- Communion.
- Post Communion Prayers:
  - Prayer of Oblation or Prayer of Thanksgiving.
  - Final Marriage Prayer provided in Series One.
- *Gloria in excelsis.*
- General Blessing.

Hymns and Readings

The *Book of Common Prayer*/Series One Marriage service can have hymns inserted into it in a similar way to the *Common Worship* service. Again, this is down to the discretion of the minister and in discussion with the couple. Having a sense of the 'shape' of the service is important. For example, it is advisable not to put a hymn or (if there is a choir) an anthem in a place that disrupts the service. Hymns and other pieces of music should be positioned so that they complement the service, perhaps coming at the end/beginning of sections of the service.

Where do the readings come in a 1662/Series One Marriage service?

The reading or readings come towards the very end of the service in the 1662/Series One services, after the marriage itself. This is another way in which the Prayer Book services are different from *Common Worship*.

If you are being strict to the Prayer Book running order, then the service (including hymns and a reading) could look like this:

- Hymn.
- Introduction.
- Declarations.
- Vows.
- Giving of rings.
- Nuptial Blessing.
- Hymn.
- Prayers.
- Hymn.
- Reading.
- Sermon.
- Hymn.
- Blessing.

Can the readings be put elsewhere in the 1662/Series One service?

Many people prefer to have the readings before the marriage of the couple instead of at the end. It is possible therefore to reflect that *Common Worship* shape, if you wish, when using the 1662/Series One Marriage service. If you wanted the reading or readings to be more prominent in the Prayer Book service, then you might want to order the service this way:

- Preface and Declarations.
- Reading(s).
- Sermon.
- Vows.
- Giving of the Ring.
- Nuptial Blessing.
- Prayers.
- Blessing.

Which readings can I choose? The *Book of Common Prayer* doesn't seem to recommend any!

The readings and Psalms that are provided in *Common Worship: Pastoral Services* (also available on the liturgy pages of the Church of England website) are ideal for use at a 1662/Series One wedding. You don't have to use the King James Version of the Bible at a Prayer Book wedding (though couples may want that). Neither are you limited to a single reading. If there are to be two readings, then one should be from the Old Testament and one from the New. If both readings are from the New, then one should be an Epistle and the other a Gospel reading.

The Prayer Book doesn't mention signing the registers!

No, it doesn't, but we all know that this is a vital thing to do. In the thinking of 1662/Series One, the signing of the registers is not something that happens in the service itself (as it does in *Common Worship*). The signing of the registers is something that's done immediately following the service.

Therefore, in a Prayer Book wedding, the signing of the registers would come after the final blessing and before the couple process out of the church.

8

Thou knowest, Lord, the secrets of our hearts
Burial of the Dead

The services and ceremonies concerned with the dying, death and the departed became a focus for the new reformed way of thinking that Thomas Cranmer championed. That is why the Burial of the Dead in the *Book of Common Prayer* is very simple, even stark. Cranmer was forwarding a new way of thinking about death through this liturgy.

The 1662 Burial service allows for everything to be done at the graveside, or for there to be a short service in church before the congregation moves to the graveside. Either way, the intention of this service was to diminish the possibility that funerals could be 'corrupted' by praying for the dead.

Structure of the 1662 Burial service

- Funeral Sentences – these are said as the body is met at the entrance of the churchyard and is taken to the grave or into the church.
- Psalm 39 and 90 (penitential Psalms) are then said.
- Lesson – 1 Corinthians 15.20 is provided.
- If the service is in church, at this point the body is taken to the graveside, where the service continues.
- Burial Sentences – these are four sentences to be said at the grave.

- Committal – said 'while earth shall be cast upon the body by some standing by'.
- Anthem – words from Revelation, 'I heard a voice from heaven, saying unto me'.
- Prayers:
  - *Kyrie*s.
  - Short form of the Lord's Prayer.
  - Two collects: the first of these thanks God for delivering 'this our *brother* out of the miseries of this sinful world' and prays for the accomplishment of 'the number of thine elect and to hasten thy kingdom'. The second collect asks that those who remain might 'not be sorry, as men without hope, for them that sleep', and it looks forward to the general resurrection and prays that 'we may be found acceptable in thy sight' on that day.
- The Grace is said as a conclusion.

The Burial service in 1662 has the advantage of being short and to the point. It has, however, some disadvantages that make using it 'as printed' a challenge. For example, the service does not allow the departed person to be named at any point; the scriptural part of the service is very long, especially the reading of such a large portion of 1 Corinthians 15; the concluding prayers are fine compositions but perhaps do not reflect the range of needs that we would want to pray for at a funeral. There are no prayers for those who mourn.

These issues are only issues if you follow the 1662 Burial service to the letter. Bearing in mind the controversies surrounding the dead in the history of the Church of England, it should not be surprising that the liturgy as printed does not contain many additional liturgical materials and prayers, but that is not to say that additional texts have not traditionally been used.

As we have seen at almost every turn, the *Book of Common Prayer* is much more flexible than it first appears. The version of the *Book of Common Prayer* Burial of the Dead that contains the variety that you might want to use if conducting a 'Prayer Book funeral' can be found in *Series One: The Burial of the Dead*. Just as the Marriage service was amended to make it more appropriate to the modern age, the Burial service was also amended and authorized for us to use.

The basic structure of Series One: The Burial of the Dead

- Introduction.
- The Service in Church.
- The Prayers.
- The Burial.
- Provision for the Eucharist to be celebrated (Collect, Epistle and Gospel provided).

The service in detail

Introduction

This first part of the service, like in 1662, is intended to begin at the entrance to the churchyard, or at the church door. Just as in the 1662 service, the Series One service can take place first in church and then graveside, or entirely at the graveside.

A greater number of Funeral Sentences are provided in Series One—nine in total—whereas the 1662 service provides only three. These are sentences taken out of the Old and New Testaments that set out the Christian hope in the face of death. They are recited by the minister as the body is brought into church/to the graveside.

The service in church

In Series One, this section breaks down into the Psalms and the readings.

Psalms

Series One provides four Psalms. Psalms 23 and 130 are given in addition to the Psalms given in the 1662 service (39 and 90). The tone of the two additional Psalms reflects the thinking behind some of the liturgical changes to the Series One Burial service – they are not penitential but pastoral.

Unlike the 1662 service, Series One provides additional texts to be said before and after each Psalm. Instead of ending each Psalm with 'Glory be to the Father . . .', Series One allows for the use of 'Rest eternal grant unto them, O Lord, and let light perpetual shine upon them.' In addition, before and after each Psalm, the *Salvator Mundi* can be said: 'O Saviour of the world, who by thy Cross and precious Blood hast redeemed us: save us and help us, we humbly beseech thee, O Lord.' This is intended to act as an antiphon (a sentence of scripture said at the very beginning and the very end of the Psalm).

Neither 1662 nor Series One seem to have a greeting?

It is true that neither of these services has an explicit introduction, when the minister conducting the funeral can greet and address the congregation in the way that most clergy and people would expect today. Because of this, it is worth considering inserting into the service (1662 or Series One) a liturgical greeting and then a short bidding to welcome the congregation and introduce the service. *Common Worship* does this with these words:

We have come here today
to remember before God our *brother/sister N*;
to give thanks for *his/her* life;
to commend *him/her* to God our merciful redeemer and judge;
to commit *his/her* body to be *buried/cremated*,
and to comfort one another in our grief.

The use of 'The Lord be with you . . .' or 'In the name of the Father, and of the Son, and of the Holy Spirit' is an effective way of making a clear liturgical beginning to the service, and the words above are then very effective in setting out the purpose of the service.

In *Common Worship*, this introduction (bidding) is followed by a collect. Again, 1662 and Series One do not provide a collect for the beginning of the funeral service, but you don't have to look far to find an appropriate collect: Easter Eve in the *Book of Common Prayer* is very appropriate or the Collect for the Commemoration of the Faithful Departed found in the 1928 Prayer Book (and also in *Common Worship*). These work very well as opening prayers for a funeral in the Prayer Book tradition.

Readings

The readings as they appear in Series One consist of a Psalm/ Psalms and a selection of Epistles. Series One provides four recommended Epistles: two passages from 1 and 2 Corinthians and two passages from Revelation.

Am I limited to the readings provided?

No. It isn't possible for all appropriate Psalms and readings to be listed, so Series One lists only some. On the liturgy pages of the Church of England's website (and in *Common Worship: Pastoral Services*), there is a full list of readings suitable for a funeral or memorial service. This is worth looking at and drawing on.

The Prayers

The readings lead into the Prayers in Series One. They follow the same pattern as 1662 – *Kyries*, Lord's Prayer, Prayers.

Additional prayers are provided in Series One to cover a wider range of needs. For example, Series One includes a prayer for 'those whom we love, but see no longer', a prayer for 'those who mourn', and a prayer for those who remain. These are shorter prayers than the ones found in 1662. If needed, they can be supplemented with additional prayers.

Where can I find 'Prayer Book style' prayers for use on these sorts of occasions?

The best source for such prayers is *Parish Prayers* edited by Frank Colquhoun (Hodder & Stoughton Religious, 1996). His first volume of prayers contains a huge variety of prayers that can be used throughout the liturgical seasons as well as prayers for certain occasions (like a funeral, memorial service or wedding). Colquhoun's book is a wonderful supplement to the *Book of Common Prayer*.

The Burial

In Series One, following the prayers, the Funeral service moves to the graveside for the burial. However, there is a note in Series One that says: 'the Burial may precede the Service in Church and the Prayers'. This means that a Series One funeral could take this shape:

- Introduction.
- Burial.
- Service in Church.
- Prayers.

In the usual shape of the service, where the burial follows the service in Church and the Prayers, the body is brought to the graveside where the Burial Sentences are said (or sung). In Series One an alternative text is given alongside the Burial Sentences. Verses from Psalm 103 are provided to be said or sung at this point. Like other texts included in Series One, this alternative is a little 'softer' in tone than the sentences.

Strictly speaking, the 1662 service, for reasons discussed earlier in this book, doesn't commend the departed to God's keeping. There is no prayer of commendation. Series One, however, provides a brief commendation at this point, just before the burial for the minister to use. The commendation and committal are contained in the same prayer (*Common Worship* has two separate prayers at this point).

Following the commendation/committal comes the anthem 'I heard a voice from heaven' and then the conclusion. Series One does not conclude with the Grace but with 'Now unto the King eternal, immortal, invisible, the only wise God, be honour and glory for ever and ever. Amen.'

What about Holy Communion at a funeral?

Series One has provision for the Communion to be celebrated by providing a collect, epistle and Gospel reading. The rubric only makes reference to the possibly of there being a celebration of Holy Communion on the day of the funeral, which does not exclude the possibility that the service in Church could be the Eucharist, after which the congregation move to the graveside.

If there were to be a Funeral Mass according to the Prayer Book, then the service might take this shape:

- Introduction:
  - Funeral Sentences.
- Service in Church:
  - Collect.
  - Epistle.
  - Gospel.
  - Creed.
  - Sermon.
  - Offertory Sentence.
  - Prayers – from the Funeral Service.
  - Prayers of Penitence.
  - Eucharistic Prayer.
  - Communion.

- ○ Post Communion Prayers.
- ○ *Gloria* (it is common for this to be omitted at a funeral).
- Burial:
  - ○ Psalm.
  - ○ Commendation and Committal.
  - ○ Conclusion.

Cremation

Because Series One was authorized in the mid 1960s, when cremation was increasingly common, the notes at the end of the service give some guidance to how the service can be adapted for use in a crematorium:

> When this Order is used at the cremation of the body, in place of the words, 'commit his body to the ground, earth to earth, ashes to ashes, dust to dust', shall be said the words, 'commit his body to be consumed by fire': and in this case it shall suffice to say one or more of the prayers at the burial of the ashes.
>
> When this Order is used at the burial of the ashes after cremation, in place of the words, 'commit his body to the ground, earth to earth, ashes to ashes, dust to dust', shall be said the words, 'commit his ashes to the ground, earth to earth, dust to dust', or, 'commit his ashes to their resting place'.

Memorial Services

Series One also provides a little helpful guidance about how the material from the funeral service could be used at a memorial service. The note at the end of Series One says: 'The Service in Church together with the Prayers may be used as a Memorial Service for the Departed apart from the funeral.' This provides you with a framework for a memorial service in the Prayer Book tradition.

For the Lamb which is in the midst of the throne shall feed them: Burial of a Child

The 1662 *Book of Common Prayer* does not provide a specific service for the use at the burial of a child. By 1928, the needs for this service had become apparent and an order of service was created for the 1928 Prayer Book. This service is now included under Series One and is authorized for use. It is very good.

The basic structure of the service

Introduction

- An additional funeral sentence is added: 'He shall feed his flock like a shepherd: he shall gather the lambs with his arm, and carry them in his bosom.'

The service in church

- Psalm 23 is appointed to be said or sung. No penitential Psalms are included.
- Mark 10.13–16 is the reading.
- Prayers are also provided that are appropriate to the occasion.
- A commendation is provided.
- The anthem is different from the anthem at the burial of the dead: 'They shall hunger no more, neither thirst any more; neither shall the sun light on them, nor any heat. For the Lamb which is in the midst of the throne shall feed them,

and shall lead them unto living fountains of waters: and God shall wipe away all tears from their eyes.'

- The service ends with the same sentence as the Burial of the Dead.

Can this service be used at a crematorium?

Yes. The same advice applies to this service as to the funeral of an adult.

What do people really mean when they say, 'I want a Prayer Book funeral'?

That is worth teasing out. It's clear from the 1662 and Series One services that a 'Prayer Book funeral' isn't a straightforward thing. Clergy and others have commonly adapted and amended the 1662 service to meet the pastoral and practical needs of the moment – a way of using the liturgy that is as old as the *Book of Common Prayer* itself.

When people ask for a 'Prayer Book funeral', it is unlikely that they mean the strict 1662 service. Even if they say they want that, when you go through the 1662 service with them they usually ask about the possible alternatives and additions. What people usually mean is a service that uses the language of the Prayer Book and that stands consciously and clearly in the tradition of the *Book of Common Prayer*, even if it isn't strictly the 1662 version. That is why Series One is such a good tool for anyone taking a funeral, because it clearly stands in the tradition of the *Book of Common Prayer* while offering the variety of options, flexibility and guidance that clergy today will find helpful if they are to minister the Gospel effectively.

Index